ONE CHANCE
for
Glory

First Nonstop Flight Across the Pacific

Edward T. Heikell
Robert L. Heikell

Acknowledgments

First, we must recognize that this story was not contrived; it was taken from sketchy historical records of a daring feat taken on by two relatively unknown early day aviators, Clyde Pangborn and Hugh Herndon Jr.

We compiled an account of the events through research of numerous Internet sources, published books, and pamphlets on the subject. The Washington State University Library, located in Pullman, Washington, maintains a complete paper file on Clyde Pangborn that his brother, Percy, and mother, Opal, donated. One most notable book was Carl M. Cleveland's *"Upside-Down" Pangborn, king of the barnstormers…first to fly the Pacific non-stop!*

We developed the account of this new book into novel context by incorporating the living fears and thrills that undoubtedly existed among friends and family during those trying times. We also attempted to interpret the relationship between the two fliers, Pangborn and Herndon. All in all, our goal was to reconstruct the story as it might have happened between 1920 and 1932.

The city of Wenatchee, Washington, has relived the event since 1931 and has established a formal sister-city relationship with the flight's departure city, Misawa, Japan, based on the flight. The commercial airport, located in what is now East Wenatchee, is named Pangborn Field. A group there called the Sprit of Wenatchee actually built a full-scale replica of the airplane *Miss Veedol* and has plans to eventually fly it around the world following the route traveled by Pangborn and Herndon in 1931. One of the members of that group, Jake Lodato, was most helpful in acquainting us with the airplane to further visualize what actually happened during the flight.

The authors visited a Moses Lake, Washington, resident by the name of Delbert Lamb, a cousin to Clyde Pangborn. Although much younger than Clyde, he knew him quite well and was actually there at the Wenatchee landing site when Miss Veedol arrived from Japan. Many of Clyde's attitudes and mannerisms resulted from this visit.

A review team, consisting of friends and knowledgeable helpers including Jack Frost, Eric Heikell, Jamie Eddie, Jake Ladato and Laura St. George helped to keep the story on track. We mustn't forget Edward's wife, Joyce, who diligently reviewed each draft, made comments, and corrected the multitude of errors that occurred during the development stages of the book.

The staff of the Washington State University Library provided excellent assistance in our review of the Pangborn papers and collections that they have stored and organized. A fantastic assimilation of logs, pictures, navigation devices, letters, telegraphs, and diaries are neatly organized in eleven feet of shelf space stored in their archives.

The marvel of the hardships and numerous life-threatening events that these two early aviators faced—and survived—is incredible. This is only a snapshot of a part of Clyde Pangborn's life. He lived on to eventually marry for a short while, but he was more devoted to the sky. He was caught up in the tragic events of World War II and played an instrumental role in keeping our allies supplied with the bombers needed to run their strategic raids. He definitely deserves a stronger place in our modern-day history books.

Contents

Foreword

We wrote this book to bring attention to two brave men who operated during the early days of aviation in order to show the practical application of air travel. Unlike Lindbergh, Post, and Doolittle of history fame, the achievements of Pangborn and Herndon were not well publicized or appreciated. Today, not much is known about either man. In their own ways, these two men accomplished what many considered an impossible feat that was not duplicated until the end of World War II.

We authors are both deeply involved in modern-day aviation and were born and raised in the region of the continental United States where much of this story was centered. We wrote this book to express our strong feelings. It's time that modern Americans recognize the brave deeds accomplished by our forefathers in bringing us to where we are today. Pangborn and Herndon were heroes, but they remain unknown to a vast majority of U.S. citizens.

Prologue

Inside the busy Tokyo Narita airport terminal, the crowd of passengers, concession employees, and crews required to staff all of the current departing and arriving flights worked their way to and from the gates. People were running and carts were whizzing by, causing a non-rushed person in a relaxed situation to be on high alert just to avoid being run over. I found it best just to crowd a wall, slow down, and watch the chaos.

Arriving flight crew members are quite tired after a flight from far off places such as across the Pacific. While most crew chores are automated, just staying alert for long periods of time closely monitoring these automatic systems is no easy task. The sophisticated systems have evolved through many years of enhancement aimed at benefiting safety, economy and passenger comfort.

Outside, it was a typical gray October day, though this month the weather was always changeable at a moment's notice. October air was often smooth but cold and full of moisture. The flying public would not expect weather-related flight delays. Automatic electronic systems had come so far and built-in flight systems were so good that flight travel interruptions were almost nonexistent in these modern times. On occasion, especially in the autumn and winter, de-icing was required before departure to assure ice buildup hadn't affected the aerodynamic efficiency of some of the critical flap and control surfaces during takeoff. Ice build-up was something to address because airplanes flew at altitudes above thirty thousand feet through temperatures far below zero for hours as they plied toward their journey's end. In addition, as airplanes approached their destinations, they must penetrate the moist air layer found below about sixteen thousand feet, which increased the opportunity for more ice accumulation. October weather was unpredictable, which was of no consequence today. But in earlier aviation, it was a month to use extra caution.

I was on a three-hour layover at this time, waiting to meet my plane for the final leg home to Seattle. While finishing my dinner at a fine Japanese restaurant, I found myself sipping a small cup of warm sake to relax my mind before catching my flight. The restaurant was beautiful and unique to my standards. It was decorated in typical Japanese style with the tables set low to the floor. A hole cut in the floor out of sight under the table allowed westerners to dangle their feet. Ornate metallic hangings of dragons, swords and historical figures often associated with Japanese culture decorated the walls. The waitresses all scurried about in their tight Kimonos using small steps distinctive of Japanese waitresses. Oriental music twanged in the background. I found it very unique and comforting—a good way to calm down before boarding the plane for the upcoming eight- to nine-hour flight across the Pacific Ocean. Nearing the end of my cup of sake, I noticed a group of four uniformed airline pilots next to me, unwinding after a long day of work. I got up to leave and greeted them as I passed. They apparently were expecting a pleasant layover in Tokyo before preparing to fly their 777 back to their homeland in the USA the next morning.

I quipped, "Oh, you must be planning to cover the *Miss Veedol* route."

They appeared puzzled and asked me to repeat the statement.

"Are you planning to cover the *Miss Veedol* route?" I repeated in a friendly way.

Obviously not pressed for time, one of the more senior men seated at the back of the table asked, "What is a '*Miss Veedol* route'?"

As the others smirked, implying I didn't know what I was talking about, the one asking the question looked at me curiously. He was undoubtedly the only honest man there.

"Who or what is *Miss Veedol?*" he asked again.

"*Miss Veedol* was the name given to the single engine Bellanca airplane that was the <u>first</u> to cross the Pacific Ocean, non-stop back in 1931. Two men by the names of Clyde Pangborn and Hugh Herndon set this record." I felt more at ease at this point as the gentlemen began to show a keen interest in what I had to say.

"Well," the same pilot said, "I guess I don't even know who or what made the first non-stop crossing of the Pacific. Everyone knows about Charles Lindbergh and the Spirit of St. Louis making a solo crossing of the Atlantic, a distance of thirty-six hundred miles, in 1927. Crossing the Pacific is nearly two thousand miles further at about fifty-five hundred miles. I never gave it a thought. I didn't think airplanes could even fly that far in 1931." The pilot's curious green eyes set in a face that reflected years of experience were riveted to my face, and he seemed very interested in what I had to say.

I told the group of pilots as I sat down next to them, "I'm sure you are all aware that we don't consider crossing the Pacific a big issue today." They could tell I was not some sort of a quack. Even though I've been on the road for several days, I always try to look professional; wearing a suit and tie, being well shaven with my hair combed. "Our commercial airline system dictates that we have two separate crews that spell each other off on longer flights like this. I know that some of you even have comfortable bunks provided for the relief crew to rest while the others fly the airplane. Today's airplanes use large modern jet engines. And the pressurized cabins help the living souls inside feel like they are at a mere eighty-five-hundred-foot elevation even though the airplane may be flying at thirty-eight thousand feet. En route flight is conducted well above any clouds and turbulent weather, offering customer comfort and minimizing pilot fatigue." I gestured to a waitress and ordered another sake as I proceeded with my story.

"The first flight wasn't nearly so easy," I continued. "I think you would be impressed with the great deal of knowledge, money, risk-taking, experience, and luck it took to accomplish it."

At this point, all four pilots seemed to have forgotten the details of their individual conversations and huddled in closer to me to hear what I talking about.

"The trans Pacific flight was done by two daring men, both driven by the strong desire to make history. One had some knowledge in aerodynamics, fight mechanics, and stunt flying, all of which played a vital role in making the crossing successful. The other had a source of money, which was of course imperative to take on this sort of aggressive undertaking.

The older pilot spoke out. "Boy I hope I don't catch any of you guys relying on stunt flying to keep our bird flying to San Francisco tomorrow—but I suspect in those days, you had to have experience in everything or you'd never make it."

"*Miss Veedol* departed Japan from a beach about two hundred miles north of here, near Misawa. It was a pretty scary situation. They were both arrested for espionage and held captive for seven weeks. Upon their release, they were given only one chance to leave and not come back. If they returned they would be immediately arrested and put into hard labor, and their airplane would be confiscated. To make the flight, the airplane was overloaded with fuel to a gross weight fifty percent above the maximum specification.

"The beach consisted of packed sand. But with the heavy load, a successful takeoff was not assured. To save weight, they off-loaded their warm clothes, emergency equipment, and most of their food and drink. Further, they were forced to take off on a moment's notice in fear that the Japanese Aero Board would discover a system they installed to jettison the landing gear to save weight and drag.

"They barely made it. When they arrived, they belly-landed on a runway cut out of the sagebrush near Wenatchee, Washington, since they didn't have any landing gear. The trip was full of events that could have ended tragically at any time. The only thing that saved them was the skill, experience, stamina, luck and a whole lotta guts that Clyde Pangborn possessed to get them home.

If you have the time, I'd love the opportunity to tell you about it."

"Well, you got me turned on," said the older pilot. "We have the time and personally I'd like to hear this story rather than to hear Bill here drone on and on about the new home he plans to build back home. I'm sure you have a long version and a short version of the whole thing—give us the mid version."

"What does it take to cross the pond to Seattle these days—in what I would say a typical, uneventful journey?" I asked. "I'm sure it is substantially less than the forty-one-plus hours it took these lads. I guess the story started much earlier than this, but let's start in the farmland near Houston, Texas, in 1923."

1

A Visitor to an Air Show

The sky was clear over Houston that early spring morning, and the eye could see for two hundred miles—if there was anything to see. The country was flat, the air was still, and the crowd was exuberant. They were about to witness an event that they couldn't have even imagined a few years earlier. The place was dusty and dirty, but nothing different from what the farmers in the crowd experienced daily. They lived out in the country, and the opportunity to see an unusual happening such as this was a welcome occasion.

Tom Webber had finished plowing his field the day before. He planned to plant a new crop of tomatoes in the field in a few weeks. While the ground was resting after the plow, he felt this would be a good chance to spend the day with his family, as the feverish late spring and summer months left no time for anything but farming. The Gates Flying Circus was in town displaying their airplanes and flying stunts in this new era of aviation. This would be a new experience for almost all who attended the show. Airplanes were the new in thing in those days, so Tom thought it would be great to take his wife Margaret and two young children, Mark and Danielle, to the show to celebrate the coming of summer.

When they arrived, they were amazed at the crowd. Parking was a nightmare when several thousand people converged in a single farmer's field. The morning was still a bit cold, but the rising sun in the clear blue sky warmed the air quickly.

The family eventually found a parking spot, and the four had to hike more than a mile to the ticket booth. They bought their tickets and proceeded into the field to watch the show. Makeshift grandstands had been constructed, but there were not nearly enough spots to seat so many people. With time, Tom found a spot for his wife to sit while he mingled through the crowd to find a good viewing location. The kids roamed freely as they were safe to do that in this crowd.

They were in awe at the stunts being performed right in front of their eyes. Airplanes with their powerful ninety-horse-power, slightly-muffled engines roared by right in front of them. Then stuntmen did acrobatics on the wings and hung by their legs from the landing gear axles.

Figure 1. Circus performer stands on head during one of the shows

This went on for more than an hour until the sights became commonplace. Their minds started to accept that these heavier-than-air machines could actually fly, and their eyes and necks became sore from taking it all in. But they were glued to the show, as the grand finale was yet to come.

The performance would end with one of the local folks doing some sort of a stunt. In this case, it was rumored that a young local woman—a girl in her very early twenties—was to jump from an airplane and parachute down to the ground.

Tom and his family could hardly wait. Who would have such bravery and guts to perform such a stunt? At last it was revealed that a local girl, Rosalie Gordon, and a pilot, Clyde Pangborn, would do the feat.

Tom said to his wife, "I don't know them now, but I bet everyone in the region will know them afterwards."

When the airplane carrying the final stunt taxied to the end of the make-shift runway, a cheer from the audience echoed throughout the farmland. There were actually three persons onboard, but nobody in the audience really understood why. The members of the crowd held their breath as the airplane lifted off of the field. The airplane circled around and around as it gained altitude. Eventually it leveled off at what seemed to be an extremely high elevation.

"I'm sure they wouldn't try the parachute thing from there!" Tom told his family. "That is just too high."

But almost before he got the words out of his mouth, Tom could see some activity from the girl and the second man over the edge of the airplane's body. Everyone in the crowd was awestruck. Tom thought, *I hope they know what they are doing—I'm not ready for my family to witness a disaster.* Then, before he could even count to three, the girl was over the side, snapped to the end of the rope, and was being dragged behind the airplane some twenty feet or so. The people in the audience felt scared, but many figured that it was part of the process of letting the girl drop from a parachute. Then a few minutes later, a number of other airplanes took off in pursuit of the stunt airplane.

Word quickly traveled through the crowd that there was a problem. Apparently, the parachute shroud line had gotten tangled, and the girl with the parachute was trapped. Other pilots took to the air in hopes of finding a way to save the girl. As numerous attempts were made to rescue her, the audience members watched helplessly and fully believed that the girl was doomed.

Tom decided he did not want his family to see this any further, so he quickly gathered them up and guided them to the exit. From there, they swiftly raced to their car and headed for home.

2

Meeting Clyde Pangborn

Three weeks earlier, the local girl, Rosalie Gordon, who wanted to be the parachutist, had a driving desire to go to a flying show, and she tried to convince her fiancé, Richard, that it was a good idea. One of Rosalie's girlfriends, Marianne, had gone to a show and told Rosalie it was the most exciting thing she had ever seen. "The fliers are so handsome, too!" Marianne had added.

Rosalie didn't think the fact that the planes were flown by handsome pilots would convince Richard to go. On an unusually cool Texas afternoon in March, 1923, Richard took her for a leisurely drive in the countryside. Fluffy white clouds filled the blue sky, and a gentle breeze blew in the open car windows. Rosalie was in such a good mood that she feared it wouldn't last. Life was good—a new secretarial job at a law firm and a handsome fiancé who treated her like a princess made everything perfect.

They drove past one of the only farms in the area and stopped for a moment to watch the cows grazing. A couple of the cows actually looked up and gazed at them as if to say, *what are you doing here?* Rosalie laughed.

"They're watching us," she said.

"It stinks around here," Richard said as he put his foot on the accelerator.

Richard was a young farm employee who graduated from high school some three years earlier. In high school, he was very popular as he excelled in the looks department and was quite active in sports. At this time he hadn't found himself yet and was in the stage where he was still waiting for that big opportunity to jump up in front of him. Cars and girls were still high on his priority list as he lived from day to day.

They sped down the road and away from the farm, and the aroma disappeared. Rosalie was hesitant but decided that it was the best time to ask him about the barnstorming show.

"Did you hear what Marianne said about those fliers she saw? She met them at an air show that was being held at Rosenberg last week."

Rosalie, too, was not far out of school. Her goal was to find a boy to marry and begin her life as a housewife. She had boyfriends before, but thought this one was serious. She and Richard plan to marry but not right away. Their wedding is planned for the summer next year. They both agreed they wanted to live the life a while and get to know each other better.

As she spoke, Richard wasn't paying any attention to what she was saying. Rosalie figured that there was too much noise from the open windows. A short time later, he stopped the car and pointed to a gigantic willow tree in the middle of a field. "Look at that beautiful old thing. I wonder how long it's been there."

"A century or more, probably," Rosalie said.

"It's magnificent, but then you know how I feel about nature," Richard said. "What were you saying about Marianne?"

"The air show, remember? I was wondering how you would feel about going to see one."

"How expensive is it? You know that I took a pay cut at work and can't afford too many luxuries."

Rosalie frowned. He was so cheap. "I think Marianne said it's a quarter per person. I can pay for it myself."

Richard grinned. "You don't need to do that. Just ask Marianne where we get the tickets."

Rosalie threw her arms around his neck. "Thank you. I know we're going to have a great time. From what I hear, you'll really be impressed."

* * * * *

On a warm Saturday morning in April, 1923, Richard and Rosalie got into Richard's Model T Ford and headed over to the farmer's field where the show was being held. Richard was very reserved and had little to say about what they were about to see. But Rosalie was very excited and couldn't keep still or stop chatting.

"This is so exciting," Rosalie said. "I can't wait. Joyce Parker went once and said it was amazing. She couldn't believe the tricks they did like flying upside down." She looked at Richard, who kept staring straight ahead. "Aren't you excited about it at all? You almost seem bored."

"None of it makes sense. Only birds are supposed to fly, not machines. It's unnatural," Richard said.

Rosalie frowned. "How can you have that kind of an attitude? Everyone thinks it's so exciting. You never know where flying might go someday. Things are advancing so fast. I wouldn't be surprised if someday people might be traveling to foreign lands on one of those machines."

They drove on in silence. Barnstorming was a phenomenon of the post-WWI years. Most passenger-carrying flights in those years were made from farmer's fields. The fields were usually adjacent to the barns, which were painted red. The term "barnstormer" possibly came from the way these events were held.

Rosalie and Richard arrived at the farmer's field, walked the typical mile from their parking spot, and found a seat on one of the makeshift benches that had been set up for the event. Everyone in the audience seemed very excited, and Rosalie heard one woman say that she'd actually gone up in an airplane the last time they were in town and it was the most exciting thing that had ever happened to her.

Rosalie leaned over the man who was sitting next to her to speak to the woman. "Do they let just anyone go up in the airplane with them?" she asked.

"Sure," the woman grinned, "for a price, they'll do anything. They take you for a test run first. And when they are sure you won't faint or get sick, they will show you all of the tricks they perform with you onboard. I can't tell you how exciting that was. I'm hoping that eventually they will let me go on a dive with them. I'm sure that, with time, I can convince them to do all of the tricks with me onboard."

"What is this 'getting sick' thing you mentioned? Is it that cold up there?" Rosalie asked.

"No," the girl said, "it is motion sickness. It is easier to get motion sickness in an airplane than it is in a car. You have to realize that your body is being tossed around in all directions in an airplane."

Rosalie couldn't help but notice how beautiful the woman was, blonde with gorgeous blue eyes. Richard leaned over and whispered in Rosalie's ear. "I bet I know why the fliers let *her* in the airplane with them."

Rosalie punched him in the arm. "Don't say that. It isn't nice. She seems like a nice girl."

Every once in a while, Rosalie noticed Richard looking at the girl, but when the show started she forgot all about it. The pilots first performed the figure eight, when they made left and right turns over pylons and then crossed over a central point between them. Then they flew upside down by slowly rolling the planes onto their backs. They rode for a long time with their heads to the ground, their bodies suspended against the safety belts. This was followed by loops, which appeared to be easy. To do a loop, a pilot had to simply push the nose down and aim at the field, then pull the stick back when he had enough speed, look at the clouds and the sky, and then look at the field again.

After the show, Rosalie and Richard were introduced to one of the key pilots, a young man named Clyde Pangborn. Rosalie was in awe, but Richard seemed uninterested.

"What's it like to be up there by yourself?" she asked Pangborn.

"I'm always exhilarated by the wind as it stings my face," Pangborn said.

Pangborn didn't seem like an overly intelligent person but a tall thin, down-to-earth practical man. He spoke rather slowly but was very precise in what he had to say. Rosalie thought he was rather good looking and would be a real "catch" for some woman but knew he was in high demand as all flyboys were at that time.

Pangborn's reply was not the answer Rosalie had expected, and she wanted to hear more.

"I like the idea of being able to fly anywhere I want," Pangborn continued. "I like the idea that people like you are so fascinated by aviation. Have you ever thought of going up for a ride?"

"Sure have. I'm sure it's very exciting!" Rosalie paused and looked at the plane Pangborn had just been flying. "I'd like to do one of those stunts, if possible."

Pangborn shook his head. "We do take people up, but our schedule is all filled up for the rest of the day. We generally don't take customers on any of our stunts, as most cannot stomach them—if you know what I mean." He extended his hand to wish her well. "It's been nice meeting you. I hope you come to another show."

Rosalie watched him walk away.

3

The Change in Rosalie's Life

For the next few days, Rosalie couldn't talk about anything aside from the flight and Clyde Pangborn. Richard grew more and more annoyed. She couldn't help noticing that something wasn't right between them, but she had no idea what it was.

One night they were listening to the large radio located in the living room of Richard's parents home. His parents were in the next room and typically gave the two younger people their "space". It was a common two-story house in those days where the furniture was grouped around the four-foot high radio that emitted a considerable amount of heat from the seven radio tubes contained inside the cabinet.

That night, the radio broadcast notice of another barnstorming show that was to take place in Kingwood the following week. Rosalie wanted to go, but she didn't know how Richard would feel about it. To her surprise, Richard immediately picked up on the radio announcement and turned to her.

"I bet you want to go, don't you?"

"Well, we had a good time at the last one, didn't we? You enjoyed yourself."

"I think you're interested in that guy, Pangborn," Richard said.

"I'm not. Why do you even say that! Besides, he's way too old for me. You know, I think you are jealous. If you were a flyer, I'd certainly ask you first—but you're not! But I do want to ask him if I can go up in the plane with him. I can't imagine anything more exciting."

Richard shook his head. "I won't let you do it, and neither will your parents. It's much too dangerous, so put it out of your head."

She stomped on the floor as hard as she could with her small low-cut leather shoes. "Now look, I'm twenty-one years old, and you can't tell me what to do. Neither can my parents. Richard, I don't know what's gotten into you lately, but I don't like it."

"You don't know what's gotten into me? All you talk about are those barnstormers. You never ask me about what's going on at the office. Don't you have any interest in my life?" He stared at her with disgust. "Your mother even told me that you've stopped making plans for our wedding!" He turned to get his jacket.

"Have you been talking to my mother behind my back?" Rosalie shouted.

"No. I saw her down town last night. I spoke to her and she told me. She wanted to go look for bridesmaids' dresses last week and you refused to go."

"We have a whole year yet! There's no rush," Rosalie said.

He yanked his jacket off the hanger. "I'll contact you tomorrow. Maybe you'll have a change of mind by then."

She looked at him, puzzled. "Change of mind about what?"

He headed for the door. "You figure it out."

* * * * *

For a few days they didn't see each other and only spoke once briefly on the phone. Then one afternoon Rosalie decided it was time they had it out and went to see Richard at home. When she got there, she saw a strange car parked in the driveway. Wondering who it might be, she knocked on the door. When no one answered, she let herself in with the key Richard's mother had given her when they went on vacation so she could take care of the cats. Rosalie was even closer to Richard's mother than she was to her own mother.

No one was downstairs, and she wondered if anyone was at home. She saw two plates and two cups in the sink. It looked like someone had just put them there as they were still wet. It appeared that two people had just eaten, rinsed out the dishes and left them in the sink to drip dry. She then decided to go upstairs although there is nothing up there but the bedrooms and a bath. The door to Richard's room was ajar, and she gently pushed it open. She was so shocked at what she saw that she thought she would pass out. She grabbed hold of the wall to steady herself and turned away from the shocking sight. Richard and the girl who had been at the airplane show were lying in his bed in each other's arms.

Richard rose up immediately. "Rosalie!" "What…"

"I guess you weren't expecting me, were you?" Rosalie said as she turned and ran back down the hall.

"I…" he stammered. "Let me explain." He got out of bed, wrapped his naked body with a towel, and ran after her. "She threw herself at me, but she doesn't mean anything to me. I swear." He stumbled as he followed her down the stairs. "Don't go before I get the chance to explain."

Rosalie turned and faced him with fire in her eyes. "Oh, go ahead. I want to hear what your excuse is this time."

He put his hand on her shoulder, but she pushed it away. "She's different…exciting. I lost my head."

"How is she exciting?"

"You know all that talk about airplane rides. She wants to become a pilot and travel around the world," he said staring her right in the eyes.

"Really?" She threw up her arms and lowered them to slap her own thighs. "When I talked about just going for a ride, you forbade me. But with her, even more aggressive flying is exciting to you."

"I love you and plan on you becoming my wife. I never wanted you to get hurt, and was afraid that just leaving the ground could be dangerous."

For a few moments they just stared at each other.

"I'm so sorry," Richard said. "I never meant to…"

She glared at him. "I'm not a fool, you know. And that's what you think I am, a silly, little fool."

"You're wrong. I don't think that at all."

Rosalie was more hurt than she had ever been in her life and couldn't stand to look at him any longer. The worst part was that she could never trust him again. And if she couldn't trust him, how could they ever get married? Maybe he had cheated with other girls and would continue to cheat after they got married.

She shook her head. "We're finished, Richard." She took off her engagement ring and threw it at him. "Good-bye!"

4

Rosalie's Big Opportunity

Dan Gordon looked at his wife, Claire, and saw the concern in her eyes. It was a gloomy day; the sky was dark, and the rain was coming down in buckets. Claire sat at the kitchen table staring out the window at the rain dripping from the gutters. Since Rosalie had broken her engagement a week earlier she had refused to leave her bedroom and had eaten very little. This was a hard time for Claire, as she was no longer in the mother role that she had treasured over the past twenty years. Rosalie was a young adult and no longer needed a mother to tell her what to do. Claire felt she was out of line to offer guidance to Rosalie unless she asked for it. Claire wanted Rosalie to see a doctor. She thought Rosalie might listen to a doctor so she wouldn't have to continue pleading with Rosalie to eat something. Rosalie refused to talk to Claire and had not left her room.

"We have to do something for her," Claire said.

Dan took a deep breath, "I know, but what?"

"Letting her go on this way could make her ill," Claire said. "Yesterday afternoon while you were at the office, I asked a couple of her girlfriends to come over. And she wouldn't even see them, not even Patty, who's always been like a sister to her. She won't eat or speak to anyone. If this goes on much longer, she'll end up in the hospital."

Dan said, "We'll have to try something. I don't like to consider it, but she has always talked about going for an airplane ride. I know where we can find one of those barnstormers. Charlie Watson knows one over at Felts Field and says he's the best."

Claire shook her head. "I don't think so. It's too dangerous."

"Charlie went for a ride just the other day, and he said he didn't consider it very dangerous at all. It was very exciting, but not dangerous. The pilot's name was Clyde Pangborn. I understand that he has a great deal of experience—learned to fly in the military. I'll give him a call and ask him a few questions, but I think it's a good idea. If we get Rosalie to go for it, possibly it will take her mind off of Richard. She needs to get back into life again, and this might be the thing that does it. What do you think?"

"Well, it is a long shot, but maybe it would be worth the try," Claire said.

Claire and Dan went upstairs and knocked on their daughter's bedroom door. "We need to talk to you, dear," Claire said.

"No, I just want to be left alone. Why can't you understand!?"

Thinking that the door was locked, Dan turned the handle and was surprised when it opened. He heard the race of footsteps and then Rosalie tried to push the door shut but was unable to. She got back into bed and huddled under the blankets.

"We have a suggestion that might help you take your mind off of the recent terrible experience," Dan said.

"What? There isn't anything to fix the situation. I'm never going to go out on another date as long as I live."

"The first thing you need to do is come out from under those blankets," Claire said. "We'd like to be able to see you when we talk to you."

"Start talking, then I'll be the one to decide if I want to come out. There's no reason to get out of bed—ever."

"You need to stop being so dramatic and come out from under those blankets," Claire said.

Rosalie sat up, watery eyed, and stared at her parents. Claire sat down on the bed and took her daughter's hand.

"Now listen," she said, "remember how much you wanted to go for an airplane ride with one of those barnstormers? Well, Daddy and I talked about it and think that maybe it would be a good idea. He's found the perfect aviator who has a lot of experience, so we know you'll be safe."

Rosalie looked at her mother. "You were always so dead set against it. That's why I stopped asking. What's different now–my broken engagement?"

"Your mother and I are worried about you and want to help you. You're still young and have your whole life ahead of you."

"It just hurts so much. I never thought I would be shunned by a another girl," she said as her father took her into his arms.

"The guy's name is Clyde Pangborn, he…"

Rosalie's face immediately brightened and she jumped up and started prancing about the room. "Clyde Pangborn? He's the barnstormer I met last week who was one of the stars in the show! Are you sure?" Her parents nodded, smiling at her sudden change of mood. "What a coincidence. He's great! Maybe he'd let me be involved with some of his stunts. Wow! When can we go?"

5

Clyde Pangborn

Clyde Pangborn was born in 1896 in Bridgeport, Washington, on the Columbia River near where the Grand Coulee Dam is now located. He inherited the aptitude to be a mechanical genius, and he enhanced this ability through a great deal of on-the-job experience and training.

His mother, Opal Lamb, came out west in a covered wagon as a child and grew up in Bridgeport, Washington. Clyde's grandmother was blessed with six children, but as a consequence was only able to bathe one child a day during the grueling wagon train trip across the country. She used the kitchen kettle to wash one child each morning before they departed camp. Coincidentally, another wagon train that was closely behind camped in the same area soon after the Lamb train departed. A five-year old boy, by the name of Max Pangborn found a kettle that was apparently overlooked by the previous train in the abandoned camp, and it contained a baby girl–Opal. The boy's family rushed the baby up to the train ahead of them to reunite her with her family. Years later, the baby girl and the young boy would eventually marry and become Clyde's parents.

Clyde's family—himself, his older brother Percy, his mom, and his dad—experienced the hardships and austere living most people suffered during those trying years in the remote areas of the west. When Clyde was only two years old, his parents separated and eventually divorced. He was moved to the small logging town of St. Maries, Idaho, with his mother while his brother was taken some 50 miles down the Columbia River to Wenatchee, Washington, with his father. His mother was later

Courtesy of the Wenatchee Valley Museum and Cultural Center #000-50-33

Figure 2. Clyde (left), his older brother Percy, and their mother Opal during an early grade school visit in Wenatchee

remarried to a man who operated a saloon in the remote logging town of St. Maries. Clyde graduated with honors from the high school there in 1914.

As a farm boy in Washington and a logger in Idaho, he was completely submerged in the operation and repair of mechanical devices. In those days, mechanical devices were very austere. If fact, that far out west, most mechanical devices were hand-me-down second hand "junk". Written instructions and machine parts were typically unavailable as transportation and communication was next to impossible. Survival required the user of all mechanical devices to fabricate, install, and fix anything that broke from scratch. Clyde's formal training, beyond his 1-12 schooling, consisted of extension courses in civil engineering from the University of Idaho. As a result, he became an assistant to the chief engineer with the Bunker Hill and Sullivan Mining Companies near by soon after graduating from high school.

He was a handsome lad at about five foot eleven. Had long, fairly straight, sandy hair which he combed back, typical of the men in those days. He was blessed with good senses which were beneficial in almost all of his activities. His sight was particularly keen. Eventually, however, he had to wear reading glasses in later years.

One key thing that he had going for him was his integrity.

Figure 3. Clyde graduates from High School and studies Civil Engineering using correspondence courses from the University of Idaho

When he spoke, everyone listened as they knew his words represented the facts.

Clyde was a daredevil and thrill-seeker, but he only got involved with activities that he thoroughly analyzed and established to be safe before pursuing them. Before he got his job with Bunker Hill, he took a job in the forestry industry near St. Maries. One of his jobs was to assure proper operation of the logging flumes that carried the huge cut logs out of the mountains in a stream of fast-moving water to a holding pond. The logs were branded on both ends in the holding pond using a sledge hammer and then moved downriver to the various saw mills. Once, Clyde successfully rode a log traveling sixty miles per hour down a water-filled flume only to land in the icy-cold log pond below. When asked to repeat his performance, his boss stepped in and announced that Clyde would never do the trick again.

Clyde was an extremely confident fellow who was not hesitant to undertake any task that others labeled as being impossible. His strong drive made him continually push the limits of possibilities.

The area was fairly remote, and national news didn't arrive there with any regularity. Clyde did hear of the work being done on the heavier-than-air flying machines, however, and he immediately developed a passion for them. In his early teens, he actually built a man-carrying glider, which he quickly crashed without being injured. He worried so much about his failure that he camped overnight with it for some time, trying to understand where he went wrong.

Drunken brawls and other unspeakable acts were commonplace around the saloon in this untamed region. Clyde learned to protect himself by necessity and also developed a strong dislike for drinking.

Clyde possessed an ideal set of attributes for his aviator dreams. He had a love for flying and the time was right. Flying was new and intriguing to everyone—it was mystical, attention getting, and wild beyond the imagination. He was both practical and technically minded. He could build or fix anything mechanical. With all of this going for him, he would often shame himself for his hate of paperwork. He felt the only paperwork that was necessary was that that contained design information—he could understand the need for that sort of written material.

A few years after Clyde's high school graduation, World War I broke out, and the Army Signal Corp asked for volunteers in the aviation field. Clyde jumped at the chance to learn to fly so he signed up almost immediately.

He joined the Corps in 1917 and received his pilots rating the following year after completing pilots training at Ebert's Field, Arkansas, and Love Field in Dallas, Texas. He was not shipped to the war front, but instead stayed in Dallas to study airplane mechanics and serve as a flight instructor.

Following the war, there was a large surplus of trained aviators and airplanes being discharged from the service. Many of the trained fliers bought up the surplus airplanes and tried to make a living in the civil environment by showing off their skills and performing a large variety of dangerous stunts. Some made it, but many were killed. Many others were simply unable to make a living at it. Clyde excelled in these endeavors and continued to practice his skills at becoming a barnstormer.

One morning in the Spokane area during the spring of 1919, Clyde stopped for a cup of coffee at a local diner frequented by other barnstormers. The greasy spoon didn't offer anything fancy, but locals enjoyed meeting there for hearty home-cooked food. Clyde sat down in a booth and opened the newspaper to the sports section. The 1919 World Series had sparked a major controversy amid rumors of a gambling fix. Eight members of the participating Chicago White Sox were all charged with conspiring to throw the Fall Classic against the Cincinnati Reds. When he looked up from the paper, the waitress put a cup of coffee in front of him, and he drank it black, then she handed him the menu. He glanced at it briefly and then put it down.

"Two eggs sunny side up, no bacon, two slices of whole wheat toast, and another cup of coffee."

The waitress looked at him for a few seconds with a bewildered expression on her face, and Clyde knew she was probably wondering what she'd done to offend him. She hadn't done anything. At times, he came off as unfriendly because he was more comfortable with machines than he was with people. It was understandable. He knew machinery like he knew the back of his hand; people were more a mystery to him.

Most people in town knew who Clyde was, and they were fascinated by his daredevil tricks. He was well respected by other aviators, too, and was developing the reputation of being capable of great things.

Figure 4. Clyde Pangborn after he was discharged from the Army Signal Corps

Clyde preferred to let his work speak for itself and said little. But he was pleased when he saw Lloyd Manning, a flier with The Gates Flying Circus, the most prestigious barnstorming group in the area, walking toward his table. Clyde had dreamed of joining the group on numerous occasions but didn't think he had enough experience.

Manning extended his hand and Pangborn shook it.

"Good morning, Clyde. Do you mind if I sit down and have coffee with you?"

"Not at all," Clyde replied. "Have a seat."

Manning sat down and looked Clyde in the eyes. "Ivan Gates and I have been talking, and we want you to join our group." Lloyd said.

"Just like that," Clyde said and snapped his fingers. "Well, I suppose it's something I might be interested in."

"Is that a yes or an I-might-have-to-think-about-this?" Manning asked.

Clyde had always been independent and didn't want Lloyd to think he was too anxious, but he knew he'd be a fool to pass up the opportunity.

"It's a yes!"

6

Clyde Becomes a Hero

Clyde flew for the Gates Flying Circus for just a short time before he was considered King of the Barnstormers. They were located in the Houston area where he served as chief pilot and was also responsible for all program PR. As such, he had to accept incoming criticism and requests.

Possibly because Rosalie Gordon was an emotional wreck, the thought of pursuing a brave adventure was appealing. She was about five feet two inches tall with thick chestnut colored hair and bright blue eyes. She wasn't a pretty girl, probably because of her slightly crooked nose, but there was something about her, a mischievous glint in her eyes that made her attractive.

Rosalie's father dove them to the airport later that day to meet Clyde, who had already been informed of Rosalie's broken engagement and subsequent depression. Clyde was ready to help as Rosalie's dad ranked high in the town's popularity list. When Rosalie and her father arrived at the airport, there wasn't really anything there highlighting Pangborn or the Gates Flying Circus. They found themselves among a number of large hanger-type buildings in which a number of men were working to build their versions of flying machines. Rosalie's father asked one of the men where they might find Clyde Pangborn. The man pointed them toward the hanger on the far end of the row.

They entered a dirty building with caked dust everywhere that smelled of oil. The room was dark with a few spotlights shining down on points where work might be conducted. To a mechanic, it was heaven. Tools were neatly arranged and organized so they could be found in an instant. In the middle of the room, a man was working on the engine of an army bi-wing airplane. This wasn't the first time Rosalie saw an airplane, but it was the first time she saw one up close and could actually touch it. Her father, too, was fascinated. Although Rosalie had already recognized him, her father asked where they might find Clyde Pangborn. The man replied, "You are talking to him."

Rosalie was careful not to push herself at Clyde, but she really wanted to go for an airplane ride to help her get over the recent break-up with Richard. The break-up upset her more than she thought it would. Clyde understood the situation and offered her a show ticket to break the ice. But after talking to her briefly, he realized that she not only wanted to go for a ride but wanted to do something more daring—possibly like jumping out of the plane in a parachute!

Even though it was customary for the Flying Circus to invite a local celebrity to perform an aerobatic stunt in each town, the mere thought of exploiting a young girl like Rosalie was unnerving. Clyde couldn't believe she would be willing to do it and hoped she'd change her mind. He was one of the best pilots on the barnstorming circuit and prided himself in being conservative on the side of safety.

He and she both agreed to meet at the temporary Ivan Gates home later that day to discuss it. Ivan was fortunate in that he had the money to live comfortably wherever he located for up to a month, as barnstorming troops were seldom in one place for long. The common house had gray mohair upholstery couches and a braided rug on the floor. Clyde sat in the living room with Ivan and Lloyd and listened to Rosalie drone on and on about how exciting it would be without recognizing the danger she would experience. Clyde tried his best to make her understand that her inexperience made it even more dangerous. After all, to date she hadn't even flown in an airplane.

"You can't be flippant about something like this," Clyde said. "We should make a practice run before the big show scheduled for the day after tomorrow."

Lloyd Manning laughed, "Bad idea. What good will that do?"

"I'll be there and be able to coach her a bit," Clyde said. "We'll see if this is something she can really pull off."

"So be it," Rosalie said. "But I know I can do this," she replied. "I've dreamed of doing it since last year. It looks like so much fun! I can jump off my roof and land in a haystack without getting hurt."

Clyde and Lloyd looked at each other and shook their heads.

"That does it," Clyde said. "We're going for a practice run first. If it's something you can handle, maybe I'll let you do it. You can be our local performer for the day."

Rosalie smiled from ear to ear, "Wow, I didn't expect that! Do you think I can do it?"

"You'll be alright," Clyde replied. "But let's practice first."

The next morning, her father was extremely nervous but drove Rosalie back down to the airport where Clyde was located. Dan had a long discussion with Claire the night before and decided they would back her desire to make the "drop". Her heart was set on it and they couldn't see a way of discouraging her at this point.

When they got to the airport, Clyde had her strap on the parachute pack and buckle herself in for her first airplane ride. He would do the flying, and his flying friend, Michael Hunt, would assist in the jump.

Michael propped the engine to get it started, and they taxied to the downwind end of the field. He then turned the airplane to the left to align it into the wind. "Let's give her hell," cried Clyde as he pushed the throttle wide open.

The airplane roared to life as it sped down the runway and soon leaped into the air. Rosalie's eyes opened wide as the ground gradually sank below them. This was her first airplane ride. She felt fear but in an exhilarating way. Gone was the feeling of heartbreak as she could only concentrate on what she was doing and what she was about to do.

Once they reached an elevation of two thousand feet, Clyde leveled off and Michael began preparing Rosalie for the jump. She was very nervous, but in no way was she about to back out. A tether was tied to the wing strut to serve as a rip cord pulling the chute out shortly after she left the plane. Once she was ready, with a little shove from Michael, Rosalie jumped off the trailing edge of the wing without hesitation. The chute opened, and she began her gradual descent toward the field below.

Rosalie was excited and extremely scared, but she also realized that there was no turning back. As she dangled from the thin ropes attaching her to the large umbrella up above, she could only pray that the ropes were secure and dependable. She didn't have time for all of the "what ifs?"

that go though a person's head in distress times like this, as she had to prepare for the sudden landing she would face shortly.

To Clyde's surprise and relief, Rosalie absorbed the landing shock with ease and completed the practice try with no problem. With that he felt more comfortable about Rosalie and considered her qualified to perform the next day.

The next morning was her chance to become the town's hero by making much the same jump in front of over five thousand people. This opportunity was beyond her wildest imagination. She was clad in white boots and a white leather flight helmet to match the white silk jumpsuit. Then she, Michael, and Clyde headed out to the Dallas, Texas, airfield. Rosalie's mother and father followed behind in their own car. Clyde tried his best to hide his apprehension even though the practice run the previous day went well.

The time came for the show's grand finally. Going through the same procedure as they had the day before, they climbed to altitude over a large crowd of townspeople. Once they leveled off, Rosalie quickly went to the trailing edge of the wing and confidently jumped. But something went wrong. Within seconds, Rosalie found herself being dragged behind the airplane at the end of a twenty-foot rope, her chute and chute shrouds tied to one of the wing struts. Obviously, she was petrified—so petrified that she was ready to pass out, her life and well-being completely in the hands of Clyde and any help that might be available.

Rosalie's parents, Dan and Claire, watched from the ground in awe. They never dreamt of the horror that would result from their decision to encourage their daughter to go on a flight with Clyde Pangborn. They couldn't stand to watch, although they were riveted to the scene above, praying for a successful end.

Later Clyde would figure out that the person in charge of the equipment had left the chute outside the night before and the cotton ropes got damp and swelled tight. At the moment, Clyde desperately tried to calm himself down so he could help Rosalie. Her skin was turning blue, and he knew he had to do something before it was too late.

Clyde looked at Michael Hunt, the young wing walker mechanic in the seat ahead of him. "Go down to the wheel axle, grab the rope, and pull!" he yelled. "Quick! Take it and pull hard."

Hunt slid over the side onto the axle and tugged hard, battling the wind and Rosalie's weight at the end of the rope. He pulled a foot, then two feet, but had to let off as the strain was more than he could sustain. Clyde asked Michael to return to his seat up front. He turned the controls over to him while he went over the side to attempt the same process since he was much larger and stronger. He found that he too could not do it alone.

By that time, the crowd was aghast and other pilots flew Flying Circus airplanes into the air in hopes of aiding the stricken performance. One pilot attempted to come up from below the girl to catch her by the wing, but he quickly abandoned that approach in fear of chopping her up in the propeller.

Then Clyde came up with a plan. He scribbled out some instructions on a piece of paper asking for the assistance of two of his favorite performers, stuffed the paper in his helmet, and dropped it overboard to the ground crew below. Within minutes, a red airplane, piloted by Jake Lodato pulled up beside Clyde's airplane on the left. Putting the wing tips together, the other man onboard, Jamie Eddie was able to wing walk his way to the tip of the red airplane onto the tip of Clyde's airplane. From there, he continued on into Pangborn's control area. With Jamie taking over the controls, Clyde and Michael were both able to work their way down to the landing gear axle to pull on the stranded girl's rope together. Little by little they were able to retrieve her until she too sat on the axle between the two men.

Clyde then worked his way back to the cockpit, leaving the other two clinging onto the landing gear structure for dear life. Using his unique skill, Clyde softly landed the airplane without causing injury to any of the occupants.

After the airplane came to a halt, Rosalie fainted and fell off of the axle. Dan and Claire were the first to reach her and splashed some of their drinking water on her face. Claire lifted her limp

Figure 5. Rosalie Gordon and Clyde (in airplane) pose with other Circus employees after daring rescue of parachutist

24

body upward to hold her tight. When she awoke, she started a grin from ear to ear.

"We made it! We made it!" she yelled.

The crowd went wild, running toward the plane, trying to get closer to either Clyde or Rosalie. Some reached inside the cockpit to shake Clyde's hand, but his arms were too weak to allow him to respond. The flying team along with Rosalie were all asked to pose for a picture to commemorate the event. They did but Clyde was physically exhausted. He could make no effort to stand straight or smile at the camera.

Word of the marvelous feat eventually spread throughout the nation. "Pangborn of the Gates Flying Circus Saves the Day," read the headlines. This event helped drive the Flying Circus to the top of the barnstorming business.

The next morning, Clyde, mostly recovered from his trying adventure, checked to see how much fuel remained in the gas tank: one pint. A double miracle had occurred the day earlier. It wouldn't be the last in Clyde Pangborn's life.

7

The Circus Grows

The publicity from the rescue made the show even more popular, and soon they had more business than they could handle. Clyde was the most popular of the barnstormers, and he developed a few more stunts to add to the ones they already had.

The show rapidly became a two-headed marvel; Pangborn running the planes, the pilots, and the stuntmen while Gates operated the business, the promotions and schedule. They were right where they wanted to be and didn't have room for a third leader—being Lloyd Manning. Lloyd was another promoter vying for Ivan's role.

At times Ivan Gate's temper was stressed beyond limits. Pangborn tried to stay neutral in the disputes but tempers flew all about him. Eventually, the Circus was starting to feel the pressure so that something had to be done.

Despite the group's success, problems between the two caused the dismissal of Manning and a new equal share partnership between Pangborn and Gates.

Clyde and Gates sealed the new alliance with a handshake in Gate's tiny kitchen. Ivan took a bottle of beer out of the fridge to commemorate the occasion, but he didn't offer Pangborn one. Instead he poured him a glass of ginger ale.

"Sure you don't want a drink, Clyde?" Gates asked.

"I saw enough of that when I was a boy, and the damage that it can do. I'm fine with this."

"I never thought I'd meet a teetotaler on the barnstorming circuit. How about a name for our new endeavor? I've got an idea. How about 'The Gates-Pangborn Flying Circus' What do you think?"

Figure 6. Ivan Gates poses at the controls of a Circus airplane—he never learned to fly

Clyde grinned, "Why not 'The Pangborn-Gates Flying Circus,' instead?"

"'The Gates Flying Circus' is a recognized name and would probably serve the purpose, at least in the near term," Ivan suggested.

"I guess you're right. Let's continue with that for the time being," Clyde said.

On any given day throughout the late 1920s, a pilot, or team of pilots, would fly over a small rural town and attract the attention of the local inhabitants. The pilot or team would then land at a local farm and negotiate with the farmer to use one of his fields as a temporary runway from which to stage an air show and offer airplane rides to customers. After obtaining a base of operation, the pilot or group would fly back over the town, or "buzz" the village, and drop handbills offering airplane rides for a small fee, usually from one to five dollars.

The advertisements would also tout daring feats of aerial daredevilry. Crowds would then follow the airplane, or pack of planes, to the field and purchase tickets for joy rides. The locals, most of whom had never seen an airplane up close, were thrilled with the experience. For many rural towns, the appearance of a barnstormer or an aerial troop on the horizon was akin to declaring a national holiday; almost everything in the town would shut down at the spur of the moment so that people could purchase plane rides and watch the show.

Although many barnstormers worked on their own, or in very small teams, there were several that put together large "flying side shows" with several planes and stunt people. These types of acts had their own promoters who would book the show into a town ahead of time. They were the largest and most organized of all of the barnstorming acts.

Several towns across the nation paid barnstormers quite well for their shows and held parties and dances in their honor. Some pilots and aerialists also obtained free room and board when they traveled. Nevertheless, the nomadic existence of barnstorming could also cause serious problems. Sometimes it was difficult for pilots to find fuel or the right parts for their planes. Other times, they could go several days without attracting a large enough crowd to make a profit. Clyde loved barnstorming, but he also considered it problematic.

This particularly became apparent one afternoon when a young man in his twenties came by to examine the virtues of becoming a barnstormer. All that he could see was the glory of flying for a living. Unfortunately, or fortunately, he met up with Clyde. Clyde was quick to tell him, "The life of a barnstormer is not romantic at all. I've slept on the bottom wing of an airplane. I learned how to sleep there without falling off. I've gone through as many as three days without sleep. There's nothing romantic about that." Before the discussion was through, the young man quietly walked away. His aspirations squashed but possibly for a good reason.

* * * * *

The Flying Circus progressed at each showing, and new stunts continued to intrigue the spectators. Clyde had a good sense of humor, and he enjoyed creating spectacle with different characters. For one stunt, an aviator dressed as an old woman would enter the passenger compartment of one of the airplanes while it was sitting on the runway and accidentally start the engine. Then the airplane would go wildly into the air. Clyde would also plant an actor dressed as a woman in the audience. He would then drag this pretend audience member into the

Figure 7. A typical Gates Flying Circus poster

passenger seat of the airplane against her will. She would pretend she wanted nothing to do with airplanes, but Clyde flew into the air with her anyway. While the crowd went wild, a dummy similar in likeness to the woman was thrown out of the plane. The crowds were impressed by these stunts and demanded more.

Clyde Pangborn, *The King of Barnstormers*, like most aviators, attracted women by the droves. But at this time, he was too busy to get serious about anyone.

All of the Flying Circus's airplanes were unique and could be recognized instantly by the blazing wing undersurface paint job spelling out the word "TEXACO" along with a white circle logo with an imbedded "T." Gates had secured a deal with the Texas Oil Company whereas he would use the TEXACO livery on his airplanes in exchange for free use of Texaco's gasoline and oil.

With the popularity of barnstorming shows, a new fad emerged in which folks would get married in flight. But the Gates Flying Circus airplanes didn't have room for a bride, a groom, a preacher, a witness, and a pilot. So, always the entrepreneur, Clyde came up with a solution to modify their Lincoln Standard Airplanes by moving some fuel tanks around to allow space for four passengers rather than three.

The first couple to be married while in flight was Frederick Simmons and Audrey Egan. They were both in their thirties and neither one had been married before, and both were anxious to get the ceremony over with because they were nervous. The preacher had just said the words "We are gathered here together…" when Frederick gasped and clutched his chest. The preacher stopped and waited. Frederick seemed to compose himself, so the preacher was about to begin the ceremony again. But Frederick then began to breathe hard, so the preacher stopped again.

Audrey let out a little squeal. "What's wrong with you, for goodness' sake?"

"It's my heart."

Clyde turned around and looked at the preacher. "What's wrong with him?"

"I think you better land the plane," The preacher said. "There's something wrong."

"No!" Audrey yelled. "Finish the ceremony. He'll be fine."

The preacher looked at Clyde, who shrugged his shoulders. When the ceremony was over and Audrey and Frederick were husband and wife, Frederick recovered instantly and Clyde landed the plane.

8

Money Problems

So much more money began to pour in from the Flying Circus performances that it was no longer practical for Ivan to keep the money under a mattress. Clyde wanted to open a bank account, but Ivan didn't trust banks. They argued about it for months while Ivan's wife, Sally, did the bookkeeping. One night Clyde came to see Ivan and Sally and found Ivan in the bedroom with that day's earnings spread all over the bed. He was counting the money and looked up at Clyde and grinned.

"I haven't even counted half and there's over twelve hundred dollars here. We're going to hit the big time fast, Clyde, my friend."

Clyde frowned. "I heard you gambled away five hundred dollars worth of last week's receipts."

Ivan was very defensive as he stopped what he was doing and looked directly at Clyde. "I lost a little on the horses," Ivan admitted. "We'll make it up next week. Don't worry," and he nervously shuffled all of the money into a stack and began putting it into a canvas bag.

"I want that money in the bank," Clyde stated affirmatively.

"I don't trust banks," Ivan said as he slammed the bag against the end table. "I want to be able to touch my money. I want to be able to look at it—he reaches into the bag and pulls out a fist full. Then he angrily shakes his fist-full at Clyde, "if we put it in the bank, we won't have any idea what happens to it, and we could wind up losing every dime."

"I want the money in the bank, and that's where it's going," Clyde insisted as he stared Gates directly in the eyes.

"You're not even talking about the real problem," Gates said. "The government keeps adding more and more rules and regulations that control what we can and cannot do in the barnstorming business."

"Well that is a whole new subject but I have to say that I've noticed that myself," Clyde said. "But I don't think there's much we can do about that. But bare in mind we'll settle this money thing soon or I'll be raising a bunch of hell around here!"

Clyde continues, "I think this regulation thing is caused by too many wannabe pilots out there having accidents and making all of us look bad—so the government gets involved. At this rate we'll all be out of business soon. Right now, it looks like we won't be able to even wing-walk without having built-in permanent supports strapping in the walk-ers. The crowds aren't going to be impressed with that."

Gates droned on, and Clyde tried to listen, but his biggest worry was the books. Although Clyde hated books, it was obvious to him that something had to be done to keep the business on the up and up.

Clyde could see that his barnstorming days were numbered and the carefree lifestyle he'd enjoyed could be over before he wanted it to be.

* * * * *

A few weeks later, Gates went on an extended vacation, and Clyde saw this as an opportunity to make a deposit in the bank. He made stacks of the bills and wrapped each stack in newspaper before putting it in a suitcase. When the suitcase was full, he took it to the local bank as though he was simply carrying his lunch pail.

When he arrived at the bank, he told the bank manager that he wanted to make a deposit and suggested they go into a back room. When he opened the suitcase and the bank manager saw the stacks of money, the room was suddenly filled with security guards, who pointed their guns at Clyde. He couldn't believe what was happening.

"What's this all about?" Clyde asked.

"Where did you get all this money?" the bank manager demanded.

"It's the proceeds from the Gates Flying Circus. I'm sure you've heard of us."

The manager didn't believe him, and before long he told one of the tellers to call the police. A short time later, two policemen arrived, one of whom had twice gone on a plane ride with Clyde.

"What's going on here?" the cop asked.

The bank manager looked straight at Clyde. "We want to know where he got the money he wants to deposit. We think it's a laundering racket."

The cops laughed, and one of them answered, "This is Clyde Pangborn; he's part of that Flying Circus out in Love Field. You know those barnstormers. I'm sure the cash he wants to deposit is part of their earnings."

Clyde nodded at the two cops. "Thanks," he said.

"What flying circus?" the bank manager asked. "What are you talking about? I've never heard of it."

"You need to get out more," the cop said. "Pangborn is an honest guy, and he's telling you the truth. The money's clean. Believe me."

9

More Stunts

The Flying Circus shows were popular, but Clyde and Ivan still felt it needed more clientele. Aero photography would be new to the public as most people could not even imagine leaving the ground.

Clyde and Ivan found out about a six-man hanging in Arizona. Ground traffic was barred from the sight because officials were concerned about crowds, as many people were interested in seeing these men brought to justice. So Clyde and Ivan took to the skies, camera in hand. They flew over the location and took a photo just as the floor dropped from underneath the dangerous banditos. The unique picture from an aerial view caught worldwide attention and brought more business to the Flying Circus.

Clyde and Ivan's Flying Circus became so successful that at one point they were using a dozen airplanes with twenty performers. The entertainers consisted of pilots, wing walkers, parachutists, mechanics, and stand-ins. Clyde, with engagements almost every day, was by far the most popular of the performers.

As these shows matured, some spectators attended the events in the hopes of witnessing an accident rather than to marvel at the performer's skill. However, Clyde's flying record was untarnished, never injuring a passenger—except for possibly himself.

One night in the year 1919 in Coronado Beach, California, Clyde planned a brave feat. He intended to climb out of an automobile as it sped down the beach and transfer to an airplane flying overhead. The speed of the two vehicles had to be exactly the same for Clyde to have any chance of success.

During practice the day before, the resort operator who hired the troop was not impressed. "It looks too easy. You need to fail the attempt several times before making the transfer—let's say you succeed on the third attempt."

So on the day of the event, two failed attempts went off as planned, and they prepared to make the successful transfer. Holding onto a safety bar, Clyde stood on a platform at the rear of the car. The driver pushed his foot to the floorboards in order to keep the car's speed at sixty miles an hour on the hard sand. The airplane passed low overheard with a ladder dangling beneath its belly like a tail on a kite, but it was a bit too far away from the platform.

Clyde, maybe being a bit too overconfident, leaped slightly to the right as he grabbed a wooden rung on the dangling ladder. Clyde was jerked fiercely up and away from the car. He held on for a moment and then lost his hold as the ladder slipped away. He fell ten feet to the ground, hitting the sand like a bullet. He rolled and bounced again and again—his eyes and nose filled with sand—his ears ringing from the impact.

Figure 8. Clyde about to leap onto ladder preceding his ill-fated display of car to plane transfer

He suffered three dislocated vertebra, some muscle sprain, and many bruises. Some of these injuries plagued him the rest of his life.

10

The Circus Breaks Up

Despite their success, Pangborn and Gates did not get along. Ivan was a promotional genius, but his hot temper and heavy drinking made him difficult to get along with. With Clyde's disdain for alcohol, the problems between the two men seemed insurmountable.

One day Clyde got a phone call from Ivan's wife Sally asking him to come to their apartment. Clyde really didn't want to go, but when she begged, he relented and left the airfield. Fifteen minutes later, when he arrived at the Gates' apartment, he could hear Ivan yelling. And when he knocked on the door, he heard Sally crying.

"Talk some sense in to him, please," Sally said after she answered the door.

Sally waited in the hall as Clyde walked into the bedroom. He found Ivan sitting on the bed, holding a gun. When Ivan saw Clyde, he stood up and pointed the gun at Clyde, then at his own head.

"Have you lost your mind?" Clyde shouted as he ducked behind the love chest that was setting near the door. "Throw your gun away before someone gets hurt!"

"I gave you a job, and that's the way you thank me!" Ivan said.

Clyde jumped from behind the chest and charged at Ivan in hopes of taking the gun from his hand.

Ivan raised his fist and struck Clyde squarely in the jaw, causing a severe compound fracture. He then raised the gun towards him and started firing.

The jaw fracture caused Clyde excruciating pain. He held his mouth closed with one hand and his jaw together with the other as he sped around the room dodging Ivan's bullets trying to reach the exit door. By the time the gun was empty, Ivan had failed to hit Clyde with a single round. In the silence that followed the shooting spree, the two men stared at each other. And then Ivan began to cry. Clyde was so embarrassed to see his friend cry that he looked away.

"Pang, I'm so sorry, so damn sorry. What the hell have I done to my best friend? I'm out of my cotton-picking mind. I'm a good-for-nothing, goddamned bastard!" Ivan said through his tears.

"You need help," Pangborn said, barely able to get the words out. The pain in his jaw had gotten worse.

"You need help, not me. Sally," he called. "We need to get Pang to the doctor. He's hurt."

"I'm not coming in there until you throw the gun out the door," Sally said from the hallway.

Ivan opened the door and tossed the gun out. Sally walked inside and took one look at Clyde and knew how hurt he was. She led him gently out the door. "I'll take him myself," she said to her husband. "I don't want to be around you when you're like this. You better think about what made you hurt your friend."

That was the last time that Sally walked into that house. She left Ivan for good and feared for her life to even gather her belongings. Ivan Gates was on his own.

Clyde spent nearly a week in the hospital before he was released. His jaw was wired shut for three months having to live on broth and other liquids that he could sip through his closed teeth. He had absolutely no desire to see Ivan during this time even though he visited the airport and flew just to stay in practice.

As it turns out, Clyde and Ivan didn't speak for weeks. The episode reminded him that death was an accepted part of being a daredevil. But all that knew him were aware that Clyde never put himself in harm's way until after he'd given the situation careful consideration. Competent people who were well-known in the business were killed on a regular basis, and Clyde didn't want to become a statistic. If he had had any idea that Ivan might break his jaw or try to shoot him, he would not have gone to his apartment.

In time new federal regulations began to restrict certain stunts performed by the Flying Circus. Then the economy began to deteriorate and people had to worry more about feeding their families not spending money for airplane rides. The Flying Circus also lost customers to competitors who offered closed cabins rather than open cockpits, which seemed more exciting to the public.

The relationship between Ivan and Clyde never returned to its previous state. Clyde never completely trusted Ivan again and didn't want to work with him. Ivan's drinking problem and associated depression affected his effectiveness and professionalism. He no longer had the drive and charisma that made up the character of this guy Ivan Gates who became so famous in the height of the barn storming era. For so many years Clyde had cherished the Flying Circus, but he could no longer see it continuing the way it was. It was less than a year after the broken jaw incident that he and other associates got together and decided to buy Ivan out for fifty thousand dollars and make plans to form a new barnstorming company. On his own, Ivan tried to establish an airplane manufacturing business but within six months, it failed. Soon after, he committed suicide by jumping out of his upper-level apartment window.

11

Clyde meets Hugh Herndon Jr.

After Ivan's death, Clyde began to concentrate on the manufacturing side of the Flying Circus, which he renamed "The New Standard Aircraft Corporation." Clyde was a major stockholder and a member of the board of directors. The Model D-24 they produced in Spokane performed well but was hopelessly out of date due to its open cockpit. It could only be used to haul passengers around an airport or to transport mail over short distances.

The whole situation frustrated Clyde. The lack of overwhelming interest in the D-24, the declining economy, the increased government involvement, and the strong competition all painted a less than rosy picture for the future. His love was flying and the thing that made that most possible for him in the past was the barnstorming business. It was hard to comprehend that all of that was coming to an end.

He was anxious to return to barnstorming, and, even more than that, new ideas began to form in his mind. He spoke about them to no one, but he began to slowly and deliberately make plans. Anyone who knew him knew that when he got an idea, it would one day become a reality. Then something happened on May 20 and 21, 1927 that made his desire even stronger. A young man named Charles Lindbergh flew solo nonstop from Roosevelt Field in Long Island, New York, to Paris, France. When Clyde heard about it he said nothing to anyone. He just thought of the many records yet to be set and realized that no one had yet crossed the Pacific nonstop.

Not to get sidetracked, he decided that it was time to put on a demonstration road show with three of his Standards and urged the corporation to support him. They agreed, and the "Empire Air Circus" was formed.

It was during one of these demonstration flights that he was approached by a stanger who claimed he could fly and wanted to join the troop. His name was Hugh Herndon Jr. Hugh told Clyde that six months ago he bought a Standard, but it was destroyed in Princeton, New Jersey. After that bad experience, he bought another one and hoped it could be included in the tour. The conversation went on for the better part of an hour, allowing Clyde to better understand this guy.

Figure 9. Clyde meets Hugh Herndon Jr.

In conclusion, Clyde found that Hugh was an aviator wannabe. Hugh's early life was in great contrast to that of his own. Hugh was raised in a big house and had everything done for him. But he later wanted to get into the in-crowd, so he asked his mother for flying lessons. His mother paid for him to attend a flying school in France during a vacation less than two years earlier. He didn't have any practical experience in maintaining his airplane, didn't know much about how to make it run, and only knew the basics of flying in clear blue skies. In addition to Hugh's lack of experience, Clyde was also concerned that the guy was a chain smoker. Clyde just couldn't understand how anyone wanting to become intimate with flying could have such a habit. Besides being dangerous around extremely flammable fluids, smoking could be nothing but a detriment to optimum performance at high altitude. BUT, Hugh's mother had money—lots of it. As it turned out, she was Mrs. Boardman, the heiress to the Tide Water Oil Company fortune.

Hugh was about the same height as Clyde, was considered attractive with short dark wavy hair and came across as having a somewhat timid personality. He would always be wearing a "sloppy" dark brown leather jacket that helped him fit into the aviation crowd. Although he didn't have what would be called a well-rounded background, he apparently had some smarts to master flying—a feat in those days.

Clyde knew that he was rapidly approaching a point in his career where he had to make some rather big decisions. If he wanted to continue flying—and he did—he would need lots of money. Even with Hugh's aviation shortcomings, he just might be the source of the money Clyde needed. *Hopefully, this guy has an aptitude so I can make a flier out of him*, he thought.

Clyde reluctantly decided that he would take Hugh on as a student and really run him through the hoops in hopes of expanding his current shallow knowledge of flying. Since Clyde was extremely versed in all aspects of flying, he felt he could teach Hugh to be a more versatile flier.

Clyde decided to make Hugh his copilot and right-hand man on cross country trips as well as some of his barnstorming adventures. He even planned for a trip to Central America to help Hugh gain experience in navigation over unchartered territory.

With all these future plans in mind, Clyde agreed to let Hugh join in with the demonstration tour. The Air Circus had a tremendously successful start; people clamored for tickets. The Air Circus performed in thirty cities, but then a tragic accident occurred in Hamilton, Ohio. Two passengers were killed, and they lost an airplane. As a result the corporation ordered them to bring the remaining airplanes back to Spokane.

At this same time, pre-depression was really taking a toll on the economy, and the number of spectators coming to the shows dwindled. Many of the fliers had to take odd jobs to keep roofs over their heads and food on the table. Pangborn had the feeling that when the effects of the declining economy did come, it would be much worse than anyone was thinking.

Then in late 1928, when Clyde returned the airplanes, he also attended a meeting of the board of directors. They informed him that the new Standard Corporation was not making a profit and, as a result, its stock price plummeted to zero. They would be forced out of business. Clyde lost a great deal of his savings on the corporation, which originally seemed to be very promising. He ordered the remaining airplanes delivered to Los Angeles, where he turned them over to past board members, who later became the founding officers of TWA.

12

Barnstorming Restart

Despite the problems of his company closing, Clyde was certain that people would still be interested in flying around a field for their first flight. He decided it was time to approach Hugh Herndon and help him realize his dream of becoming a barnstormer. Clyde telephoned Hugh, and Hugh answered the phone almost as if he had been expecting the call.

"Are you still interested in barnstorming?" Clyde asked.

"Is this Clyde Pangborn? My mother said you might call."

"She's a determined woman," Clyde said, "Is she still ready to put up some money—I'd say ten thousand dollars?"

"She'll wire me the money tomorrow, if I ask her," Herndon said.

With Hugh's mother's money plus another ten thousand dollars Pangborn withdrew from one of his accounts, they were able to buy three airplanes, a Packard Limousine, and other accessories from a defunct barnstorming corporation. The two men excitedly named their new company, "The Flying Fleet." Both were anxious to get started for different reasons—Hugh felt as if he'd finally achieved a dream, and Clyde felt he was one step closer to realizing his dream—flying a record around the world time and flying nonstop across the Pacific.

The Flying Fleet didn't have a good beginning, but it was still able to meet all its financial obligations. Much of their operation was centered in central Washington around Ellensburg and Yakima, where Clyde often visited his friend, Charlie McAllister. Charlie and his brother,

Allister, were coincidentally rebuilding a Standard Airplane in Yakima, where Charlie had opened a flying school just a year earlier. He was one of the first aviators in the state of Washington and held a license signed by Orville Wright.

Charlie, like so many of the early aviators, had big ambitions. The world was ripe for breaking aviation records, and he had his own ideas. On the drawing board was a design of a glider he would name the "Yakima Clipper." Clyde couldn't help but visit Charlie during this design process to offer his guidance.

"I can't build her for several years yet. But if the design is right, I can break the world endurance record for gliders," Charlie said.

He planned to launch the glider off Rattlesnake Ridge south of Yakima using shock cords in an attempt to catch the wind lift prevalent in that area. As a backup, a team of volunteers would stay in the valley below during the night to light small fires marking the edge of a landing strip in the event that the wind stopped and a landing in the dark was necessary.

Clyde knew what made an airplane fly, and he had a great deal of advice to offer Charlie. The two would work until the early morning hours on the design. Working with Charlie only added to Clyde's practical experience that would be of value in his future ventures.

Unfortunately, the Flying Fleet hadn't been in business very long before an accident and the Great Depression did them in. After a show in Pecos, Texas, a family with one very pretty girl showed up and pleaded with one of the fliers to take them up. The girl was flirting with the flier, and he succumbed to her charms. There were too many for the flight, but he put them all in the front cockpit anyway. His engine had not yet cooled off from the day's activities, but it had been shut down for the night. Although he got the engine started, his fickle mind forgot that the shutdown procedure had already been conducted, which included closing the Lunkenheimer fuel valve. Soon after takeoff, the fuel-starved engine caused an emergency. Instead of following the very strict emergency procedure and finding an emergency landing spot straight ahead, the pilot attempted a steep turn back to the field. The plane stalled and crashed, and the pretty girl, who was Miss West Texas, was killed, and the others were injured.

The pilot had been fired the previous day, but he was asked to stay on until they found a replacement. By having four passengers and himself in the airplane, he violated the maximum passenger load, and the insurance was waived. The financial burden fell on the Flying Fleet—some five to seven thousand dollars.

The Flying Fleet stayed in business for thirteen months, but the accident was a big issue. The great depression and the increased competition that used more modern equipment added to their problems. They finally stopped performing in February 1930. During their existence, they carried one hundred twenty-one thousand passengers and booked one hundred cities in thirty-six different states. After the final show, they stored their airplanes but later used all but one of them to pay off the hanger rent.

Clyde and Hugh used the remaining airplane to continue their search for new flying adventures. Hugh was retained as a partner, as his mother continued to fund their travels.

13

In Boise

Meanwhile, in early spring of 1930, near Boise, Idaho, an older couple had just bought a ranch and was in the process of moving in. Steve and June Bronson had wanted to buy a larger farm for more than twenty years, and they finally found one that they could afford. Although they couldn't get much for their old farm, the depression lowered the cost of the larger farm to a point they couldn't resist. They couldn't believe their luck. Although the place had been established for more than fifty years, the Bronsons scurried about it as though it was a new toy. They planned to modernize the buildings by making major changes as time permitted.

The ranch had been vacant for three years because the previous owners had been unable to make a living from the land or find a buyer for it. When the owners met Steve and June, they were extremely elated. Steve felt guilty, as the owners almost gave the place away. To the owners, it was worth it just to get out from under the burden during those hard depression years. For the most part, Steve and June were retired. But they soon became so active working on their new farm that their son and daughter, who thought their parents should take things easier, complained that they were busier than ever. They planned to use goods from the ranch to help augment their small pension, so they began the process of moving in with gusto.

The main out-building was a large barn used to shelter the livestock as well as a place to store farm equipment, feed, and outsized household goods. It was a typical design for the 1920s, a gabled structure with an attached shed on each side. Since the ends were the longest dimension of the floor plan, the sheds supported the rails for the huge doors, which slid both ways from the center to open the barn up wide. The doors had been stuck wide open for years, and Steve planned to address the problem in the near future to protect the stored hay.

The entire upper floor was mounted nearly twenty feet above the ground and served as a hay loft. At seven o'clock one morning Steve moved one of his Jersey cows into the large open barn for the morning milking. It was an early spring day, and the air was crisp and clear. The barn was dirty, and cobwebs crossed throughout the interior due to the long vacancy. The cow was placed in one of the many old milking stalls with her head locked in a stanchion made of sliding wood boards. Steve sat on one of the one-legged stools for milking and leaned his head against the cow's thigh for stability. This position was also helpful as Steve would know if she was unhappy and about to kick. This was new to Steve, as they had only been in operation for a few days. It was a refreshing change, with the clean air whistling through the boarded interior structure. Birds fluttered among the rafters and sang as though to welcome the new day.

On the other side of the barn, makeshift hutches had been assembled rather hurriedly during the past week to accommodate the one hundred laying hens June brought over from the previous farm. The hutches were tight but still allowed the chickens to escape into the large pen, which offered them some freedom. On this morning June was gathering their first laying of eggs to prevent them from getting broken in the primitive hutches.

It was peaceful and extremely quiet. As the morning progressed, they could hear the moaning of a gasoline engine far over the horizon. It sounded a lot like a car but had an unusual beat to it. They had never heard anything quite like it. June stopped gathering the eggs and listened more closely.

"Steve, do you hear that? What is it?"

He looked up. "Sounds like some sort of an engine."

They went back to what they'd been doing, but not for long. Within minutes the noise grew so loud that the Bronsons became alarmed and dropped their chores to search for the source. To their surprise, they spotted a bi-winged motorized "flying machine" in the sky such as they had only seen in newsprint, headed right in their direction.

"It's going to hit the barn," Steve said and grabbed June. They headed for cover.

Steve was trying to comfort June, who had begun to cry. "It's going to destroy the farm," she said.

"Not, the entire farm, dear, but it might destroy the barn. Right now I am more concerned for Betsy and your chickens. "Stay down and stay calm. Hopefully it will be over in a few minutes. We're going to be fine."

Steve and June watched as the flying machine dove straight for the broadside of the barn. Its descent ended in a flare three feet from the ground, and it began to zoom parallel to the ground through the cavern-like barn cavity, only touching the cobwebs hanging from the ceiling.

Chickens flew everywhere, and the cow bucked in its stall and kicked over the partially filed bucket of milk. Every rodent in the place ran from its hiding place.

Steve exclaimed to his wife, "Are you alright?"

"Sure, I'm alright, how about you?"

"I'm fine. What an experience! I wonder what that was all about?"

"We may never know," June said. "I just hope it's not a regular occurrence around here."

Steve remarked, "I never dreamed of seeing one of those new fangled flying machines—especially way out here in the country. I'd like to see one of those up close—but under different circumstances of course. If we continue to see them this way, we'll never get any work done."

* * * * *

In the airplane, Clyde and Hugh were just as surprised as the Bronsons. They looked at each other, and for a few seconds neither one said a word. They just looked back at the chickens scurrying around in circles.

"I checked this place out two weeks ago, and it was abandoned!" Clyde yelled over the engine. "It has been abandoned for years and seemed like a safe place to do this practice flight. Maybe we should have checked the place out a few days ago, but I never thought anyone would be living here."

Hugh was terrified. "We're lucky we came out of that alive!"

"I've seen a lot worse," Clyde said. "You need to calm down. Take a look at all those chickens. I bet that's something you've never seen before. I am sure that we caused those folks a few bloody eggs, which normally happens whenever chickens are spooked just before they lay them.

"We had better find a place to set down and then go and have a talk with those folks," Clyde continued. "I think I saw them run, screaming, into the house. We need to explain what happened. Let's pray we didn't do them any real harm."

"I don't think we did, but we do need to talk to them," Hugh agreed. "I'm sure we terrified them."

There was plenty of room in the countryside, and it wasn't long before they landed their Curtiss JN4D Trainer, better known as a "Jenny." They taxied back closer to the old barn and shut her down.

Figure 10. The Curtiss Jn-4 "Jenny" bi-wing airplane

The Bronsons had come out of the house and were standing on the porch, gazing out at the two aviators.

"Well, good morning," Steve said. "We never imagined in our whole life that we would be introduced to one of those flying machines in this manner. You caused us quite a good fright!"

"Good morning," Clyde responded. Hugh nodded. "Are you folks okay? We're sorry for the scare, but this place has been abandoned for quite a few years."

"We're fine," Steve said, "just a little shaken. We just moved into the place a few days back. Haven't done much yet to make it lived-in."

The two were obviously upset, but at the same time they were impressed by their first encounter with an airplane—right on their own farm! They had already decided to be congenial with the pilots under the circumstances.

"The two of you look like you could use a good breakfast," June said. "I'm making pancakes, eggs, and sausage. How does that sound?"

"It sounds great," Herndon said and looked at Clyde. "Aren't you hungry, Pang?" he asked.

Clyde was silent.

"My wife's won awards for her pancakes," Steve said. "I wouldn't miss a chance to try them, if I were you."

Clyde spoke, "We're really sorry about scaring your livestock."

The foursome headed into the house. Soon they were all sitting around the table enjoying June's pancakes.

"They are the best I've ever tasted," Hugh said.

Clyde nodded. "We are extremely sorry for what happened and hope there's no real damage to your barn or livestock. We're barnstormers, and we're traveling to Washington to visit my mother in Wenatchee. We came this way a few days ago and no one was living here. We both thought the place looked abandoned."

"He's right," Hugh said. "There was no sign of life earlier, and it looked like no one had lived here for some time."

"We thought we could make a practice run through the barn," Clyde said. "We didn't think we'd be causing anyone any trouble. If you and your wife are interested, here are a couple of tickets for free rides." He handed them to Steve. "We'll be up this way again in about a month."

June's face glowed as she asked, "Can you get a couple of extra tickets for our son and daughter?"

"Sure, that shouldn't be a problem," Clyde said, "Here are a couple more."

Steve's eyes lit up. "I never dreamed of going up in one of those flying machines. It should be great fun. Sure, we'll take you up on it." He laughed. "Our son wants to learn how to fly and daydreams about being a pilot. I told him to stay in college and keep studying accounting."

"I had the same dream," Hugh said. "And look where I am. Let your son have his dreams."

Clyde said to Hugh, "He's just trying to be practical." Clyde turned back to Steve. "But your son needs to understand this is a tough way to make a living."

"How did you get involved in flying?" Steve asked Clyde.

"I got involved as a result of the war," Clyde answered. "The Jennys were surplused by the government and, not surprisingly, bought by the men who were trained to fly them."

"Were you one of them?" Steve asked.

"I was," Pangborn smiled. "I fell in love with flying before I was in high school. But the practical aspects of airplanes had still not been discovered. In civilian life, airplanes became no more than a man's toy, where competition could be arranged between fliers. They'd compete to see who could do the best rolls, fly faster near the ground, fly upside down, do the most daring wing walking, and parachute from the highest altitude."

"It sounds dangerous," June said.

"It can be if not done carefully, and it can be something like a lottery," Clyde said. "It's also quite profitable, which is what attracted so many aviators. Not only could they show off their amazing skill, but they could charge bystanders five to ten dollars for a ride, which meant they were making more money than they had ever imagined."

They finished breakfast, and then Clyde and Hugh left with the promise that they would see the Bronsons again soon. The two aviators returned to the Jenny. Hugh spun the prop to get it started and then got in, and the two took off.

Later, Clyde felt pleased with the way the conversation with the Bronsons had gone. He was glad he hadn't given away that much about the barnstorming business, done any real damage, or frightened them too much.

14

Pangborn Starts to Dream

A new idea began to form in Clyde's mind—setting a new around-the-world speed record. He still planned on being the first pilot to cross the Pacific, but he was thinking about doing the around-the-world thing first. The speed record could be achieved more easily than a flight across the Pacific, as the record was currently held by the slow balloon-type airship, *Graf Zeppelin*, which had taken twenty-one days, seven hours, and thirty-four minutes. At the current time, Clyde knew of seven teams that were working to beat this record, but none of them knew what it would take to achieve success. He did. He had as much knowledge and flying experience as any of them. But he needed a lot of money, a winning plan, and a good flying partner to pursue it further.

Hugh was the only man Clyde thought of that met most of the qualifications to be his partner. Clyde was still not confident about whether or not Hugh was as clever and as daring as a man needed to be for such an undertaking. Clyde also doubted Hugh's skill as a pilot. But he did know that Hugh had the financial means to make this happen. Between purchasing an airplane, fuel, and supplies, and paying for living expenses, the bill would be staggering.

Clyde made some preliminary plans and studied the tactics being followed by other contenders. Clyde's knowledge and expertise with airplanes was in high demand because only a small number of people could even relate to this type of work. Few could fly airplanes with the exceptional skill he possessed, and even fewer could maintain an aircraft in the condition necessary to take them safely into the air.

His skill as an aviator would make it possible to change his career into some other line of work, but excitement combined with a relaxed work schedule were an important part of any job that might interest him. If he and his inexperienced friend, Hugh, could come up with a plan, money might not be an issue—as long as they could convince Hugh's mother to back the venture financially. Clyde had a lot of ambition and the burning desire to become "someone" in the aviation field, in much the same way as Charles Lindbergh, whose fame and admiration were insurmountable. Clyde read about the ticker-tape parade Lindbergh was given in New York City and dreamed about the same thing. He knew that the way to achieve notoriety was to set some sort of aviation world record. So, the idea for an around-the-world speed record became an obsession with him.

He decided it was time to tell Hugh about his plans. Clyde asked Hugh to meet for lunch at a nearby café, where they often went to discuss upcoming events. As usual, Clyde was early and Hugh was late. Hugh had just had a fight with his new girlfriend and couldn't decide whether to break things off with her or not.

"I didn't come here to discuss your problems with women," Clyde said. "If you didn't juggle so many of them at once, you might be able to figure things out."

Hugh laughed. "You wish you had my problems."

"No, I don't. We have something important to discuss." Clyde said. "Pretty soon we can both see an end to our careers as barnstormers. I really hate to see that happen because barnstorming has been good to both of us, but there's an end approaching."

"I know," Hugh replied, "all those new rules and regulations."

"Yes, and other things. I've been thinking about recent developments in aviation and am convinced that airplanes definitely have a future beyond barnstorming and fighting wars."

Hugh took a bite of his cheeseburger. "I couldn't agree more. There are so many possibilities, like taking people from one place to another and not just around an airfield."

Clyde nodded. "You may not be the best pilot in the world, but you are a bit of a visionary. We need to pool our skills and knowledge and set a new world record. Think about it, Hugh. Can you imagine our names in the record books? I think we should make an attempt at beating the around-the-world time record."

"I don't know, Clyde," Hugh said. "That would take a lot more navigational and weather skills than you and I have put together."

"We may be weak in those areas, but we know as much as anyone else and all we need is the determination that we can learn more. By the time we're ready to make the flight, we'll know everything we need to know," Clyde said.

"With a lot of hard work, it could be possible," Hugh said.

"Yes, and we would also need an airplane with exceptional capabilities. I think there are some excellent designs out there capable of such a trip." Clyde looked directly at Hugh, "Maybe we can ask your mother to help us out financially. I know she told me she would do anything she could to help you out in your endeavors."

"Yes, she did say that," Hugh smiled. "But it would take several years of planning and preparation to make such a flight a reality. When do you think we could plan on making such an attempt?"

"Within a few months," Clyde said emphatically as he pounded his fist on the table. "To be first, we have to get started immediately and stay focused. I have a plan. There are a number of teams planning an attack on the record out there right now—all with the philosophy that it would take the fastest airplane to win."

"Is that true?" Hugh asked.

"The en route time is made up of a lot of parts—the en route flying time is only part of it. There are a lot of other aspects, like the amount of time spent on the ground taking on fuel and making rest stops. I believe that if we have an airplane with extreme long-range capabilities, and the ability to get heavy fuel loads out of short unimproved airfields, we can beat the race by making fewer stops."

"It sounds like a good plan and a stupid idea all at the same time," Hugh said. He takes out a cigarette and lights it, then jumps up and sets on the table. "Let's give it some thought. First, we need a good airplane that meets those qualifications. But there's no time to build a special design. So what airplanes are available with the proven reliability and the performance you think we need?"

"I think there are two airplanes we should consider, Hugh. They are the Bellanca Skyrocket and the Ryan NYP," Clyde said. "Lindbergh's first choice was the Bellanca, but he was discouraged when the Bellanca Company officials insisted on one of their employees accompanying him on the flight. Lindbergh wanted no part of them and went to Ryan instead. I hope that Bellanca learned their lesson and will be more accommodating to us."

"You'd think they would be, but you never know," Hugh said.

The waitress brought the dessert menu, and Hugh ordered apple pie ala mode. Clyde just had coffee. He rarely had dessert and wished Hugh would do the same, because they needed to keep their weight down in anticipation of the flight.

After the waitress brought Hugh's dessert, Clyde continued the conversation. "The Bellanca Skyrocket has a tremendous load-hauling capability with its large wing and a powerful Wright J-6 engine. The range isn't as good as I would like it to be, but more fuel tanks can be added at the factory. Right now all the fuel is stored in the wings, but maybe there is some way that fuel can be added elsewhere. I am sure that there is plenty of volume in the plane centrally located near the center of gravity."

"What kind of modifications did Lindbergh make when he went over to Ryan?" Hugh asked.

"They were substantial. He added fuel tanks high above the engine and eliminated the forward-looking windshield and replaced it with some sort of periscope. Our mission isn't a nonstop flight, and we will be doing a great deal of multi-leg navigation."

"Yes, we'll need good foreword visibility to know where we are and where we're going," Hugh said.

"I have experience with the Bellanca airplane and am a bit biased in their direction—if the company will cooperate with us," Clyde said.

Hugh began to figure out loud. "The cost of a Bellanca Skyrocket, fuel tanks, fuel, emergency equipment, extra navigation gear, lodging, food, and other stuff would cost a fortune—I'd say around one hundred thousand dollars."

"It would be an expensive venture, but then fame is expensive. Do you think your mother would be willing to help?" Clyde asked.

"I don't know, but we can ask her. I know I'm excited about it, and I hope she will be too."

That afternoon they went to see Hugh's mother. They arrived at a plush mansion and were greeted by attendants at the door. As they walked through the enormous doorway, the room before them was large and well-lit. Chandeliers and stained glass windows twinkled from above. A maid led them into the living quarters, where they were seated in overstuffed chairs and offered a glass of champagne while they waited for Mrs. Alice Boardman to arrive. She soon walked in with two personal attendants, who took care of her dealings and financial matters. Clyde explained his plan and included the role that he intended for Hugh. He would not only be a copilot, but a full partner in the operation.

Not surprisingly Mrs. Boardman agreed to give them the money they requested quickly to finance their plan. Hugh's aunt was also there and agreed to give them an additional fifteen thousand dollars. They were in business!

Before they left, Hugh's mother said, "It's worth every cent of it. If you succeed, you will both be heroes."

Clyde and Hugh both smiled and nodded.

They quickly climbed into their car and left for their humble surroundings in Clyde's hanger. It was there that they drew up papers and organized the "Around the World Corporation" to be headquartered in a hotel suite located in New York City. Hugh would serve as president of the corporation, and Clyde would hold a lesser management position, even though the success of the flight would depend solely on his skill, knowledge, and experience as an aviator. Employees of the corporation in New York would maintain status of all pertinent information on other competitive teams, other available records, other prizes, and provide the public relations needed to support the effort. They would also provide assistance in obtaining appropriate permits and applications as well as organize travel for those who might be needed to support the flight.

In their hanger, Clyde emphasized that the next few months would be a busy time for both of them. There was so much to be done that neither of them would have time for anything else. Long days and short nights would be a way of life if they were to be successful. Hugh agreed.

In the March 21, 1931 issue of the *New Yorker* magazine, Hugh was quoted as saying, "We will make the flight under three conditions. We will take no subscriptions from anybody. We will pay cash for the things we have to get, including gas and oil. Finally, we will make the most careful preparations that have ever been made for a long-distance flight."

15

Clyde Meets Diane

As promised Clyde and Hugh returned to Boise ten days later and went directly to the Bronson farm, landing the plane safely near the property but far away from the house and barn. When they approached the house, they smelled the aroma of freshly baked bread, and Hugh grinned.

"Ever smell anything better?" he asked.

"Apple pie," Clyde said and poked his friend in the ribs.

Clyde had been in an exceptionally good mood since Hugh's mother agreed to help them out financially. He felt so certain that they would be successful that he'd even made plans about how he would spend the prize money, which was completely against his character.

Clyde knocked on the door, and shortly, a young woman in her early twenties answered it. She had dark blonde hair cut into a bob and bright blue eyes, which he thought made her very pretty. What was even more important to him was that she looked intelligent, not like one of those silly women who constantly giggled over movie stars and flyboys. Behind her stood a young man, possibly two or three years older with the same blue eyes. Maybe they were the Bronson children.

"Can I help you?" the girl asked.

"I think we're here to see your parents."

"Oh, of course, come on in," she said.

They stepped onto the porch and a moment later heard the sound of a truck coming up the graveled driveway. Steve and June stepped out and waved at them.

"We saw the Jenny," Steve said as he walked up the stairs. "June got all excited because she hasn't been able to talk about anything but going on a plane ride since you left."

"Are you Clyde Pangborn?" the young man asked.

"My son, Michael," Steve said, introducing them. "My daughter, Diane," he indicated the young woman. "We told them about your visit, and they've been dying to meet you."

Clyde looked at Michael and Diane. Clyde had given Steve flying tickets for all four family members earlier, so he was expecting some comment from Michael and Diane—but neither one of them said anything. Michael and Diane went and sat down at the kitchen table, and Clyde and Hugh kept looking at each other, both thinking the same thing at the same time. Should they tell the Bronsons about the trip? Both Clyde and Hugh were so excited that they didn't think they could keep it secret.

"June just baked some bread, and I know you'll want to try some with some fresh churned butter. Why don't you make a pot of coffee to serve with that, Diane?" Steve said.

She smiled, jumped up and immediately started its preparation. Within minutes they were enjoying the delicious bread with freshly brewed coffee. Clyde and Hugh looked at each other and grinned.

"You've been staring at each other since we sat down," June said. "Is there something you want to tell us?"

Clyde grinned, "Only if you can keep it a secret."

"Sure," Steve said. "It sounds important."

"Hugh and I are planning to break the around-the-world record," Clyde said. "We hope to leave in six weeks."

The Bronson family was stunned.

"That sounds dangerous," June said. "How will you eat, how will you sleep?"

"I don't think that's what they're concerned about," Steve said. He looked at the two pilots. "How dangerous is it?"

"Every flight is dangerous," Clyde said. "But I'm one hundred percent convinced that we'll make it."

* * * * *

Steve and June Bronson were then invited to go for a ride. Clyde was sorry he couldn't take Michael and Diane too, but he told them he would do his best to get them up the next time.

Clyde and Hugh gave them an experience they would never forget. First Clyde performed the well-known loop-the-loop and barrel roll maneuvers. When he was finished with those maneuvers, he wing-walked, and then to the Bronson's surprise another plane appeared as if out of nowhere and Clyde performed a plane to plane transfer with another pilot.

"Where did he come from?" June asked. "This has to be the most exciting thing that's ever happened to us."

"I have to agree," Steve said.

"Yes, but I'm going to have a long talk with Michael about becoming involved in it. They're risking their lives."

Clyde overheard the conversation but didn't say anything. He was there to entertain them, and that's what he was going to do. He then performed his specialty—slow-rolling his plane onto its back and flying it upside down. It was this stunt that had given him his famous nickname—Upside-Down Pangborn. He then landed in a vacant field several miles from the farm.

Once on the ground, the Bronsons were out of breath. They stepped out of the plane and hugged each other, then turned around to find Clyde and Hugh grinning at them.

"Would you like to go again?" Hugh asked.

"I don't think my heart can take it," Steve said. "How many times a day do you guys do this?"

"I've never counted," Clyde said. "But I know one guy who took ninety-eight people from the same town on rides. People love to go for plane rides with barnstormers."

"It is a lot of fun, and scary too." June said

Soon they were airborne once again and on their way back to Bronson's farm. When they got there, Diane had lunch waiting—grilled cheese sandwiches and tomato soup.

"My favorites," Hugh said.

Clyde laughed at him. All foods were Hugh's favorite. But Clyde realized that a family was one of the things missing from his life. The only family connection he had was his mother and brother. He had been unable to make it to Washington last week, but would do so before the around-the-world flight.

He found himself sitting next to Diane listening to her discuss nursing school. She was studying to become a nurse in the new pediatric field, which Clyde thought would be difficult, especially if the children are terminally ill.

"What if you get too close to a child who's not going to live?" Clyde asked.

"That's already happened once, and it is very hard, almost impossible. But you have to stay strong and never give up hope for the parents' sakes," Diane said.

Clyde shook his head. "It makes what we do seem inconsequential," he said.

"Not at all," Diane said. "I think what you do is very important. My friends and I have discussed this new obsession with aviation, and we think that someday people will travel around the world by airplane. It could even affect medicine eventually in some way."

He smiled at her. She was a visionary, and he hoped to see her again, maybe even before the flight. Clyde saw that Steve and June were watching them and smiling.

* * * * *

A couple of nights later, Clyde showed up in Boise again, and he and Diane went to see Charlie Chaplin's *City Lights*. They laughed through the movie and were still laughing when they pulled up in front of the farm. Even though he was over thirty, Clyde didn't have much experience with women and wasn't very good at making conversation. The only thing he felt comfortable talking about was aviation, and he was thankful that Diane kept asking him questions about the around-the-world flight.

"Aren't you the least bit frightened?" she asked.

"I'm more frightened sitting here talking to you," Clyde said. "Just like I was when I was sitting with you in the movie theater."

"Little old me, I'm harmless. No, I mean you're doing something no one has ever done before."

Clyde shook his head. "Others have done this before. I'm just trying to break their record."

"Still, it's quite an accomplishment." She opened the car door. "You take care of yourself, Clyde. Try not to take any unnecessary risks."

He knew she meant well, but on the flight he and Hugh were about to take, that was impossible. He watched her walk away, and when she reached the porch, she waved at him and he waved back. Clyde made a promise to himself that he would see her again.

16

Finding the Airplane

A couple of weeks later, Clyde and Hugh sat in the Wilmington, Delaware, offices of Bellanca Aircraft Company to negotiate for a new airplane. The reception room was obviously designed for a very large company. The decor was very businesslike, a receptionist sat at a desk at the front, and soft but not overdone couches graced the perimeter of the room. As they sat, Clyde was pleased that, since the airplane only sat two people, there would be no possibility of any other passengers.

"There should be no threat that the company will want to send one of their employees with us," Clyde said to Hugh.

Hugh replied, "I don't think that they could find an employee stupid enough to want to go with us anyway."

They both laughed.

While waiting to be called in for their meeting, the phone kept ringing almost nonstop, and the receptionist barely had time to catch her breath. Both Clyde and Hugh wondered what was going on.

"Maybe another flier interested in buying a plane to make an around-the-world trip," Hugh said.

Clyde shook his head. "The last thing we need to do is get paranoid. I'm sure it's something else entirely."

"You're probably right," Hugh said. "I just can't help thinking about it. We're so close. And I'd hate to think of something spoiling it for us."

"Nothing is going to stop us," Clyde said.

The phone rang again, and the receptionist looked up at them. "You can go in now. They are ready for you."

Clyde and Hugh looked at each other. They both wore new suits paid for by Hugh's mother, and both were thankful they looked clean and neat and weren't wearing their usual flight gear.

"It's important to look your best," Hugh's mother had said.

Clyde knew she was right. They both got up and made their way into the office of the president of Bellanca. What a place! It was a big office with a big desk. One side sported a picture window from where you could overlook the entire airfield. The other walls were decorated with pictures and paintings of aerodynamic themes. There was even a picture of Charles Lindbergh, even though everyone knew the guy flew a Ryan airplane to Paris.

The man beside the desk, Joe Ruggerio, was probably in his sixties. He had silver hair and was decked out in a cowboy hat. Clyde had no idea why the president wore his cowboy hat since they weren't out west, but somehow it suited him. There were two other men standing next to Joe at the meeting, but Clyde had no idea who they were. Both seemed younger and were also casually dressed.

Joe spoke first. "Gentlemen, let me introduce you to the founder and owner of Bellanca Aircraft Company, Mr. Giuseppe Bellanca. Giuseppe built the first airplane in Italy and came to America to get more involved with aviation."

Giuseppe reached out his hand to shake those of Clyde and Hugh.

"You boys are striving to accomplish something very significant for the world of aviation, and I am honored you have chosen Bellanca to be a part of it. I told Joe I want to take a personal interest in your airplane to be sure it does everything you want it to do. If you have any questions or need any special support, don't hesitate to contact me."

Clyde and Hugh were excited to meet someone with such stature at Bellanca. Giuseppe came to America twenty years earlier, worked with other designers, and opened his company just three years prior—about the time Lindbergh contacted them about his planned Atlantic trip.

"Thank you, Mr. Bellanca. Everyone please have a seat," Joe said.

At the meeting they decided that they would not use a Skyrocket model. Instead, because of the large number of modifications, they would rename it the Bellanca J-300 Long Distance Special. In addition to the two 108-gallon wing tanks, a floor mounted tank holding three hundred twenty gallons of fuel would be mounted behind the seats with a small floor remaining beside and behind the tank. One hundred sixty-five gallons would be stored in a belly tank along the centerline.

Joe Ruggerio, a man of few words said simply, "More fuel."

Clyde, another man of few words, nodded. "Yes, and that's the most important thing. But I can see that there is still a little room to add more. Why didn't you put tanks in those areas?"

Joe replied, "We wish we could, but the airplane structure and engine just could not handle this extra weight. Maybe some day in the future, the airplane can be beefed up to take advantage of this added fuel."

The engine would be fed by gravity from the two wing-mounted tanks. All additional fuel would be supplied by pumping the fuel located in the lower tanks to the wing tanks using an extremely reliable manually operated wobble pump. The pump could be easily operated from the aft compartment location.

Joe went on to explain, "Also as a weight-saving measure, you must be informed that we compromised the size of the wobble pump. First of all, we are using a wobble pump because it is very reliable and it has a long and slim shape allowing it to fit well out of the way."

For emphasis, he held up a typical wobble pump for all to see and operate on the table. It had a comfortable handle mounted on it allowing the operator to shuffle the slider back and forth. He was trying to make it very clear that the importance of this pump could not be taken lightly. Success of the trip depends on this pump and the person operating it.

He went on to explain, "We could put in a pump that will shoot up to a pint of gas into the wing tanks with each stroke. Sure, it would take a lot of energy per stroke, but at the same time, the pump would be quite heavy. By using a small pump, each stroke might transfer only something less than a cup. I suspect transferring one hundred gallons might take from eight hundred to one thousand strokes. That seems like a lot. But then again, you guys will have time on your hands—so I think it makes a lot of sense to save the weight."

"Oh, yes," he said, "Lots of fuel and low weight. That is the secret to your success."

"As an additional weight-saving measure, no doors will be installed," Joe said. "There will be two zippered openings in the top and sides behind the body fuel tank. The cab windows will be the primary means of pilot ingress and egress from the airplane."

Clyde took a deep breath. "Of coarse you guys know a lot more about airplane design than I do, but I was curious what measures you would take to cut the weight out of the airplane. I guess we'll have to get used to crawling in and out of the forward windows."

"We gave it a lot of thought, and this seemed to be the best way. Oh, and by the way, you will both be flying this airplane longer than your own capacity can stand. There will be a urine disposal tube mounted through the wall with a funnel on the inside for that purpose," Joe said. "Your friend here doesn't seem to have much to say." He indicated to Hugh.

"Pang's the expert on this stuff, and I defer to him," Hugh said. "I'm just kind of along for the ride and hope to be of some help."

Clyde frowned, not really understanding what Hugh was up to. He has been in on this thing almost from the beginning. Then he said "We should all be built like Hugh. Being young, slim and flexible, he should be able to slip into and out of those windows in a hurry. No kidding though, he'll have plenty to do," Clyde said, "and he has an opinion on everything. Right now, he may be more worried about all of those legal papers back home."

Joe continued on his talk. "The plane would be powered by a Wright J-6 Super inspected engine that would push the cruise speed up to ninety-five miles per hour. And Clyde, you know this, but don't let your speed get above one hundred and sixty mile per hour. That is the placard speed where above that, we don't know what will happen. Possibly the worse situation is if you let your speed build up and at the same time you pull up using high load factors. I don't know how disciplined of a pilot you are, but be careful not to get into a situation where you might do this."

Joe sat down to rest after making such a forceful talk. "This airplane, like all airplanes, has its limits. Most are common and well understood such as the maximum design gross weight. For this airplane you don't want to load the airplane to anything over six thousand pounds.

"If the plane is operated beyond these limits, we can not assure the integrity of the airframe," Joe said.

Clyde shook his head in the affirmative. "Of course. I understand." He looked at Hugh, who was fidgeting in his seat. Then he remembered that after the meeting Hugh was planning to see Rose, his New York girlfriend. Clyde wondered how Hugh kept track of all the women in his life.

Clyde told Joe, "We are going to embark on a trip never before accomplished in an airplane. There is no way of really forecasting what we might encounter. It wouldn't surprise me if we'll be forced to exceed some of those design limits. How much margin might we have?"

Joe explained, "You have to understand, God did not make all spruce wood equal. The design sample that was used had strong wood and weak wood, and the structure is based on strength characteristics of the weakest wood—so, possibly, the airframe is generally overbuilt. On the other hand, there might be wood out there that is weaker than the weakest in our samples. If you exceed any of the limits we specify, we cannot be responsible and you had better pray for greater beings to protect your safety."

"I guess what you are saying is that we just cannot encroach on these limits," Hugh said. "If we do, Clyde, we'll just have to call on help from the *Pangborn Factor* as our greater being."

Clyde laughed and said, "I don't want to be responsible for any problems, but we can use the name just to remind each other of potential problems."

The airplane would be delivered with all the best flight and navigation equipment available, including a pioneer earth induction compass, a periodic compass, a pitch indicator, and the usual altimeter, airspeed indicator, tachometer, rate-of-climb indicators, and a gasoline level gauge for each of the gravity-feed wing tanks. The fuel gauges would be simple but highly reliable glass see-through tubes mounted up high in the wing roots—hard to see but very positive in smooth air. Clyde was grateful to have all of them.

Even interior and exterior lighting was specified. All light bulbs were to require minimum power so that electrical power could be supplied using dry cell batteries—batteries to be supplied by the purchaser.

"This should be a very functional design, giving us the performance needed to be very competitive on our around-the-world record attempt." Clyde said. "The fuel load is considerably larger than the four hundred gallons carried by the Ryan NYP used by Lindbergh. Our objective of reducing the number of fuel stops can be met with a high degree of certainty."

Joe smiled. "That was something we were determined to do for you."

"There are two major consumables in this airplane," Clyde said. "While the airplane carries seven hundred gallons of fuel, it also carries fifteen gallons of vital lubricating oil automatically injected into the operating engine." He laughed. "Maybe we can get further support from The Associated Oil Company if we name the airplane after their popular Veedol motor oil that we'll be using. The bird needs a name anyway, how about *Miss Veedol*?"

"I like it," Hugh said. "It has a unique sound."

Joe explained, "Fabrication of the modified airplane could not be made as quickly as you had hoped for, but the airplane should be ready within several months."

17

The Airplane Is Complete

In six weeks, Bellanca Aircraft Company notified them that *Miss Veedol* had rolled off the assembly line. The two packed up their supplies and traveled to Delaware to check out every detail of the airplane. Rollout was not only a big event for Clyde and Hugh; it was also a big event for Bellanca, as delivery was not an everyday event. The Bellanca Company had already test-flown the airplane using their own pilots, checked out all the systems, and cleaned the airplane so that it was absolutely spotless. They placed it in the middle of the delivery hanger floor on top of a bright red carpet.

When Clyde and Hugh arrived, they were given a quick briefing and led to the hanger's main door. They were treated like royalty—an employee offered champagne, and Joe led them down a red carpet to the hanger door. Pride and anticipation gripped the pilots. As the door opened, it was clearly evident that they were both breathless. There sat *Miss Veedol* square in the middle of the floor on a red shag carpet. Spotlights were arranged to highlight the major features and give the impression that all the airplane needed now was a pilot.

"It's beautiful!" Clyde exclaimed. "Look at it, Hugh."

"I can't take my eyes off it," Hugh said.

"I can't get over how impressive it is," Clyde said. "Look at those lines. Your guys who are in charge of the aerodynamics must have spent a lot of over time to get that right! It looks like one screaming machine—and

I like that international orange color we picked—and the scrolled *Miss Veedol* logo is a real standout."

The two walked closer to look at the details. They peeked in the windows.

"I'm surprised how small the interior is considering the huge exterior," Clyde said.

"Most of the available space was used in fuel stowage as you both requested," Joe said. "There is still a little room available, but not much."

"Other than that, everything's great," Hugh said. "Right down to each nut and bolt. Look at that panel—it sure is impressive–and the instruments—nothing but the best!"

Clyde grinned. "Learn to love every part of it, Hugh. It will be our home for a long time. We'll be glad we have every instrument there and wish we had more.

"Here is a unique feature, Hugh," Clyde remarked. "The four wing struts have been made into small wings by adding more chord and an airfoil shape to them. Bellanca has them aligned with the airflow during cruise so that the oncoming air hardly knows they are there to reduce drag. At low speed during takeoff and landing, the struts are at an angle of attack to add more lifting surface to the airplane, allowing slower speeds."

Hugh responded, "Where did you learn all of this stuff, Clyde? I thought they were just to support the wing."

"They are, but since they have to be there, Bellanca devised a way to make them more functional. Because of the high lift created, a large nose-down pitching moment probably results," Clyde went on to explain. "There are two ways of counteracting this moment. One is to create negative lift on the tail and the other is to position the internal weight further aft."

Clyde wasn't trying to impress anyone, he knew this stuff. When the airplane is taxed to give everything it has, he'd probably have Hugh dancing around inside like a jester, just to have his weight located in the optimum position.

"During our operation in carrying heavy loads, we'll have to load the airplane far aft to help decrease the downward lift needed by the tail."

They were then led to the waiting room as the Bellanca crew rolled the airplane onto the ramp for checkout and training flights. Both Clyde and Hugh were quickly cleared on flying the airplane. Their previous experience in flying different airplanes made checkout in the Bellanca a snap.

They flew the airplane back to New Orleans. Once there, they flew the Bellanca through a large number of conditions to get more experience in handling the new design. Clyde was very impressed with the performance and handling characteristics of the Bellanca with one exception—an exception that he felt was important. The takeoff performance was not as good as expected for lifting the heavy fuel loads out of short fields—a primary concern if they were to take advantage of the slower cruise speed design. The only way to get the performance was to get a larger engine, which would decrease the cruise fuel efficiency of the airplane unless it was flown at higher altitudes. The improved takeoff performance would allow them to lift off with the large fuel loads, more than offsetting the penalty in cruise fuel efficiency.

Figure 11. Miss Veedol awaits final delivery at the Bellanca factory

After taking into account all of the factors regarding performance, cost, weight and balance, time delay and certification, Clyde and Hugh agreed that they would install a new Pratt and Whitney WASP 425 engine. The 9-cylinder, 1340-cubic-inch displacement WASP was a proven design. During the five years of operation, it had developed the reputation of being extremely reliable. It only weighed 650 pounds but produced exceptional takeoff as well as power at altitude. It was widely used by many aviation greats, including Charles Lindbergh and Amelia Earhart.

18

Final Preparation

When he returned, Hugh seemed to be working at home or at least somewhere else, as he was never available for consultation. Details of the flight plan, supplies, and airplane preparation were completely left up to Clyde. Occasionally, Hugh would stop by to get signatures, but that would be a quick stop in and then he would leave within ten minutes.

Clyde was concerned about Hugh's lack of attention to detail and tried talking to him about it without much success. Clyde could only guess that as they approached their departure date, Hugh was preoccupied with his new actress girlfriend and was never around when Clyde had something he wanted to discuss with him. He wanted to be with Diane too, but all they had time for were daily phone calls, which Clyde never missed. Diane understood how important the flight was, and he wished Hugh understood that he needed his help in making critical decisions. One night when Hugh decided to stay home, Clyde knew it was time to go directly to his house and find out first hand what was going on.

He traveled to Hugh's house and knocked on the door. There was no answer, so he knocked again. Finally, Hugh answered, dressed in his evening robe and holding a drink in his right hand.

"What are you trying to do, Hugh, destroy our plans?" Clyde asked sternly. "There's only one thing we should be concentrating on now—our planned record flight. There should be no serious involvement in anything else—not even a girl!"

ONE CHANCE for *Glory*

"I guess I'm not supposed to have any kind of life," Hugh said. "What about you? You're on the phone with Diane all day long."

"That's not true, and you know it. There are things we need to talk about, and early tomorrow is as good a time as any." Clyde stomped away, leaving Hugh in the doorway, looking at him.

The next day, Hugh showed up and had to spend all morning getting caught up in the latest details that Clyde had developed. Although they were somewhat at odds with each other, the two pilots continued to make their plans and were convinced they could beat the twenty day around-the-world time record set by the *Graf Zeppelin* two years earlier. Clyde spent most of his time concentrating on the technical and navigational details, while Hugh focused on supply requirements, finances, and legal paperwork. Together they gathered food, clothing, survival equipment, and other necessities needed to cross the miles of water and barren/untamed territories expected en route.

On occasion, Hugh would bring a contract and other paperwork for Clyde's review and signature. Clyde had little interest in these details and would often sign the papers without taking the time to review them. The two depended on each other to do the right thing in his area of responsibility, since there was no extra time for them to pay much attention to what the other was doing.

Often it was necessary to keep track of the other teams who had already begun their quest to beat the record. Any airplane able to endure the grueling long trip could be the winner. Clyde and Hugh's objective was to set a record that could not be easily broken.

"We have to take the time to check and double-check everything down to the smallest detail," Clyde said. "We need to have every detail on engine and mechanical preparation, navigation details, fuel availability, field conditions, rest stops, and other items that are critical. Engine timing, for example, can also be critical. The smallest timing error can cost a lost of fuel efficiency that could mean a failure of our mission."

"Pang, you have to ease up on yourself a little. We've done all that over and over again."

"Maybe you're right, but this is important. And for now, it's all I can think of. We also need to check the timeline for all fuel stops. They must be carefully planned and even rehearsed to assure optimum performance. While we plan to minimize the number of stops, the time penalty associated with descending, landing, refueling, and making mechanical checks must be thoroughly studied. An error in navigation en-route can kill us too, and we both need to understand all this. It may seem tedious, but it's vital."

Hugh nodded. "I understand it all. Really, I do. I want you to have confidence in me."

Clyde had already lost confidence. He knew that Hugh was not making the record attempt his number-one priority and suspected his mind was somewhere else—possibly on his girlfriend. He was quite disappointed that he had to depend on this guy who he trained and nurtured over the past half year to do the job they promised his mother—the person who financed the trip—they would do.

He said. "Alright then Hugh, we are almost ready. We have the best equipment available, so it's all up to us."

* * * * *

Their departure date was fast approaching. Clyde found himself again making all of the arrangements alone. For some reason, Hugh was not available. Clyde guessed that Hugh was again busy with his girlfriend, and that made Clyde angry. He had to make all the decisions by himself on Hugh's behalf. When Hugh finally showed up, Clyde was well-equipped with notes for his review. Most of Clyde's decisions were acceptable to Hugh, but some adjustments were necessary. Only a few days remained to make last-minute changes and load the airplane.

19

The Big Shock

Right in the middle of all this activity, the front door flew open and Lyle Wymer, a long-time friend of Clyde's and the city editor of a local newspaper, came into the room brandishing a newspaper. Lyle was usually calm and reserved, but his eyes were ablaze as he sped across the room to where Clyde was seated at his makeshift desk.

"Have you seen this?" he asked as he slammed the newspaper on the table. "The world-circling time record that you've been preparing for has already been broken by two guys Named Wiley Post and Harold Gatty flying a Lockheed Vega. To cross the Pacific, they made a stop at Fairbanks, Alaska, and Edmonton, Alberta, in Canada much as you two plan to do. It took them eight days, fifteen hours, and fifty-one minutes. They'll be honored with all sorts of celebrations, even a ticker-tape parade down the streets of New York—that's planned for tomorrow."

Clyde grabbed the paper and held it up to his face to read it himself. Sure enough, his goal had just been achieved by someone else. His mind went into a whirl. *What does this mean? We are ready to do that trip and should have been there in New York instead of Post! But we would have done better than the eight day, sixteen hour record. We would have cut the number of stops in half. We can still beat that record!*

This was bad news for Clyde and Hugh. Everything that they had been feverishly working toward in the past several weeks was in jeopardy.

Then Clyde said, "Not all is lost. It just means we need to regroup. We've already planned a trip around the world, we have an airplane, and we aren't going to change our plans. By God, Hugh and I are going to fly around the world and beat the record just established!"

"Do we have any other options?" Hugh asked.

"No. I think we should delay our departure for a few days," Clyde said. "For now, let's look at their 208-hour record they set and see how good it is. We know that the record was set by a very good team with a faster airplane. If my calculations are correct, we can cut six hours off of that time using our slower long-range airplane concept."

Hugh nodded. "It makes sense. For sure we won't get any credit for doing nothing."

"We need to get back to the original plan," Clyde said. "We'll have to increase our emphasis on making every second count. We're no longer trying to beat a record set by an airship. We have to beat a record that is now eleven days shorter."

A day before their departure from New York City, Hugh arrived for the final loading with Clyde. He brought some papers for Clyde's signature. As usual, Clyde signed them without looking them over and went back to work.

"Clyde, I think I should tell you what's been going on during the last few weeks. I've been busy making plans and finally made the plunge. Mary Ellen Farley and I got married last week."

"You what?" Clyde exclaimed. "You've been chasing that chick around all this time when you had the responsibility to plan, train, and prepare for possibly the most important event of your life? What the hell is going on in that pea brain of yours—if anything?"

"I know it sounds bad," Hugh said. "I promise that I'll keep my marriage from having any further impact on our record attempt."

Mary Ellen Farley was an actress who caused Hugh Herndon to commit to marriage. He wasn't really ready for marriage, perhaps he never would be. But she was able to keep his mind off of the stressful ordeal of planning for the around-the-world trip. Would Hugh be committed to her? Possibly, but she would be generally in the background. She would be a reason for him wanting to return home during their record attempt, but not the reason for "pulling all stops" to get home early.

About four weeks after the successful Wiley Post and Harold Gatty record, the Pangborn and Herndon team was ready to go.

20

The Last Chance to Relax

Clyde would remember that as a young boy living in the deep woods in Idaho, he spent hours lying on his back imagining himself pulling back on the control stick of his own airplane. In his mind he could feel the liftoff, and then he would soar over the mountains and up into the clouds and the blue sky. Then, like the eagles he watched diving for their prey, he'd point his airplane's nose down. Down, down he would go, his eyes watering from the wind, his heart beating with excitement. He imagined pulling back on the control stick easily—just in time for the wheels to kiss the earth. He cherished the freedom of flying and the opportunity it provided in getting around Mother Earth.

Figure 12. Clyde and his mother, Opal

He promised himself he would make one final trip back to Wenatchee to see his mother before he departed on his around-the-world record attempt. He could do this with ease but would lose several days flying there and back. To him, it was very important to see his mom before such a significant venture.

He was sitting in the living room of his mother's small house in Wenatchee thinking about the past and realizing he was a lucky man.

All of his boyhood dreams had come true. Opal came into the room and handed him a glass of juice.

"Dinner will be ready in ten minutes," she said. "I made your favorite, Sauerbraten and dumplings."

"I'm sure I'll enjoy it, Mother. I've never tasted cooking better than yours."

Opal smiled. "It's too bad your friend couldn't come with you. I wanted very much to see him again."

"You will...one of these days. He's a newlywed and wanted to spend this time with his bride. You know how that is."

"What about you, Clyde? Is there anyone in your life?"

"Actually, I just met a very nice young woman. A nurse by the name of Diane. Hugh and I almost destroyed her parent's barn—that's how we got to know them. We got to talking, and I found her very interesting. Not the usual kind of a girl who goes after flyboys."

"I hope I get to meet her someday," Opal said.

"You will. Right now *Miss Veedol* is the only woman I'm serious about, and she's a beauty." He took a photograph out of his back pocket and showed it to his mother. "Have you ever seen anything prettier?"

"It's your dream come true, for sure," Opal said. "Just like this coming flight is. You were always so daring, Clyde, even as a boy. Remember as a young man what happened when you wanted to transfer from an automobile to an airplane?"

"I sure do." Clyde grinned. "They all thought I was nuts. That's an interesting thing to bring up now, Mother," Clyde said. "Are you trying to tell me something?"

"Only that you need to be ready for anything," Opal said.

"I don't look for any trouble. If our good luck on the weather holds out, the flight will be ridiculously easy. Don't worry."

On his way home from Wenatchee, Clyde made a stop at Boise to see Diane. When he got to the farm, he was met by June, who was on her way into town to do some shopping. To Clyde's disappointment, Steve was away for the day and wouldn't be back until late evening.

June smiled because she knew he was really there to see Diane and not Steve and her. "She's on duty at Saint Luke's until four. I can drop you off there, and you'll probably be right on time to join her for lunch."

Clyde blushed a little. "I'd like that, if that's no trouble for you."

"I'm going right past the hospital. Just sit tight. I'll be ready to leave in a few minutes."

Within a few minutes they were on their way to the hospital. June was still talking about the flight he'd taken them on and told Clyde how much they really enjoyed the opportunity to fly with him.

"A lot of people feel that way," Clyde said.

June smiled. "Michael wants you to take him on a ride as soon as you can," she said.

"Sure. I'll take him and Diane."

They stopped at a stop sign and she turned to him. "How dangerous is this flight you're going on? We've been reading about it in the newspapers."

"It's not dangerous at all. I know what I'm doing, and so does my copilot. Besides, it's been done before, and those pilots came back safely. We're just looking to break a record."

The hospital was on Bannock Street, right in the middle of the city. It had been there for more than thirty years and was considered the best hospital in the state of Idaho. Diane was in her last year of nursing school and was already spending most of her time on the floor, not in the classroom.

"She's a natural at what she does," June said as they pulled up in front of the hospital. "Her father and I are so proud of her."

"You both have good reason to be," Clyde said.

"She should be in the cafeteria around this time. If you don't find her there, ask at the fourth-floor nurses station," June said.

Clyde and June hugged briefly, and he got out of the car and headed for the front door. Like most people, he found being in the hospital stressful. He followed the signs and soon found himself standing at the cafeteria door, but when he looked inside, he saw two male doctors who were obviously engaged in a serious discussion, maybe about a patient. Diane was nowhere to be seen.

He had the elevator operator take him to the fourth floor and quickly found that there was more than one nurse's station. The nurse at the first station had no idea where Diane was, and there was no one at the second station. By the time he got to the last one on the floor, Clyde was starting to feel more than a little frustrated.

"Do you know where Diane Bronson is?" he asked.

"She's with one of her patients in room 411," the nurse said. She looked at him quizzically. "I've seen your picture in the paper. Aren't you…?"

"Charles Lindbergh," Clyde answered. "Yep, that's me."

The nurse laughed. "I'll find out who you are. I'll get Diane if you want me to."

"No, I want to surprise her, if it's okay," Clyde said.

The nurse nodded, though Clyde wasn't really sure if what he was doing was all right. But he continued down the hall until he came to room 411. He peeked inside and saw Diane leaning over a crib staring down at a baby about a year old. She seemed like such a natural care-taker. Clyde knew that he felt different about her than he did about all the other women he met, most of whom just threw themselves at him because he was a flier. Diane was different and had her own life and her own interests. He took one step inside the room and called her name softly. She turned around and beamed.

"Clyde, I never expected to see you. I thought you'd be busy preparing for your flight."

He smiled back at her. "Well, I am. But I had to stop and see the prettiest girl I've met in a long time. For luck, you know."

"You came just at lunch time, so if you don't mind cafeteria food, why don't we go down there and see what they have to eat today. The food's actually pretty good. Just stay away from the chicken ala king."

He took her arm and they headed for the cafeteria. When they got there, they saw that it was crowded. And for a few minutes Clyde thought of suggesting they go to a restaurant, but he decided against it since he didn't have the time and he thought she probably didn't either. They both ordered tomato soup and grilled cheese sandwiches and then found a table.

Clyde took a bite of the sandwich. "The food's pretty good," he said. "Probably better than anything I'll have starting a few days from now."

Diane looked up at him. "Just how dangerous is this venture you're going on?" she asked.

"Your mother asked me the same thing, and I'll tell you the same thing I told her: it's not dangerous at all. My biggest worry is that we won't break the record."

"That sounds like you aren't too confident that you'll be able to," Diane said.

"No, I am. It's just that you never know with these things. I also have to take Hugh into consideration, and he's kind of a loose cannon. You know what I mean."

"I do. My brother has been reading everything he can find about it, and so has my father," Diane said. "It's almost like they're going to be up there with you."

They looked at each other and the expression in his eyes told her that he'd rather have her with him than her father and brother.

"I appreciate the interest. Your father and brother are good men. Your whole family…"

Their eyes met again. "I only have a few minutes before I have to be back on the floor," Diane said. "I wish we had more time to talk, but I have a patient who's just recovering from a rather severe surgery, and I want to check on him."

"Your work is so important," Clyde said. "Were you just in his room? How's he doing?"

"He's doing very well, but then young children usually do better than adults."

He paused. "I hope I see you again after the flight."

She smiled at him. "Oh, you definitely will."

21

First Leg Around the World

On July 28, 1931, Clyde and Hugh flew *Miss Veedol* to Roosevelt Field in Long Island, New York, and arranged for the start of an attempt to beat the existing around-the-world speed record.

They were both anxious to get started. To witness the departure and say good-bye to her son and Clyde, Hugh's mother had chartered a pace plane to watch from above and partner with *Miss Veedol* en route for a number of miles. *Miss Veedol* was filled with fuel and given a thorough check-up to assure everything was working properly. Once ready, Clyde and Hugh crawled into the cab windows and began the starting procedures.

Figure 13. Clyde and Hugh ready for takeoff

Clyde nosed the orange Bellanca down runway Number One before an audience of onlookers who cheered him and Hugh on. Clyde made sure the calibrated timepieces they had with them were working correctly. An automatic timepiece calibrating device utilized the time signal given by any broadcasting station to provide calibration automatically once every twenty-four hours.

The number one airstrip was not paved and had created a problem for some earlier attempts to gain adequate speed for liftoff with heavy loads. The aviators could still see the remains of an earlier attempt by Rene Fonck, a French flier, when he failed his takeoff and plunged over an embankment at the end and burst into flames. Both pilots onboard were killed. Clyde tried not to think of such fatalities as he sat in the pilot's seat looking down the runway.

The runway was the shorter of the two runways. But it was headed more into the wind and would serve as a good test for *Miss Veedol's* exceptional takeoff capability. The drop-off at the end was several feet, ending up on the longer, paved runway, Number Two.

After Clyde released *Miss Veedol's* brakes, the airplane lumbered down the runway—accelerating more slowly than the rate Clyde considered adequate. Soon, it became painfully apparent that the takeoff was not going to happen in time with the heavy load they were carrying.

Clyde turned to Hugh, who was primed and ready for his command. "Pull the dump valve!" Clyde yelled.

Hugh quickly opened the large valve, which dumped hundreds of gallons of fuel almost instantly. As a result, *Miss Veedol* was able to lumber into the air, narrowly missing a hanger not far from the end. Then *Miss Veedol* circled the air field, landed, and was quickly made ready for another attempt—but this time from the longer paved runway, Number Two.

Clyde's skill as a flier was credited for the successful recovery from the earlier attempt. He was personally credited for saving the flight by Hugh's mother, Mrs. Boardman, who landed during the time required to prepare for the second attempt.

Nine minutes before they were to take off, another flier coincidentally named Boardman took off on a flight plan to Constantinople.

Lacking any further difficulty, *Miss Veedol* then left for the initial nonstop flight to England. Pangborn tracked a more southern route than Boardman because it seemed they could avoid much of the bad weather that typically prevailed over the northern route.

Hugh could barely be heard over the drone of the engine. "Why hasn't anyone ever thought of that before?" he shouted.

"Don't know," Clyde shouted back. "But I'm certainly glad that no one has."

"Maybe there's a reason no one ever has," Hugh said.

"We'll find out."

Almost immediately, they encountered fog that persisted all the way across the Atlantic Ocean, which was a surprise to them. Clyde couldn't help thinking that Hugh had spoken too soon about possible trouble.

Clyde looked at his copilot and frowned. "Maybe you shouldn't have said anything," he said.

Hugh shrugged his shoulders, "maybe."

Clyde leveled out at twelve thousand feet as the temperature was rapidly dropping well below freezing. The airplane would fly more efficiently at higher altitudes plus he could avoid gathering excessive airframe ice. He looked over at Hugh, and for the first time he noticed something strange. It seemed that Hugh had a pale tint to his skin and was somewhat slow in his responses.

"Hugh, are you alright?" he asked.

"Sure, I feel fine—I already miss having a cigarette, though," he responded. "We typically haven't been flying this high. Why are we doing this?"

"We have to," Clyde said. "For these long-range segments, we need to squeeze everything out of this bird that we can. She wants to fly even higher—somewhere around fourteen thousand feet and above. Is that alright?"

"Oh, sure, I'll just have to get used to it. Higher altitudes might make it harder, though."

Clyde had been up for more than twenty-four hours and in a very stressful situation, so he knew he wasn't in the best mood. What he needed more than anything was some sleep. He found he had no choice but to turn the controls over to Hugh to fly at a fixed heading and altitude. He wondered if he could trust Hugh to fly the airplane under the zero-visibility conditions with Hugh being less than one hundred percent in physical—and probably mental—condition.

"Can you take over and fly this fixed heading and altitude okay, Hugh? I've got to get some rest. I'm about ready to fall asleep at the wheel."

"Sure. I don't know how you were able to keep up with it as long as you had. I'm lucky that I was able to get some sleep back at New York during our wait."

Clyde then swung the controls over to the copilot's side, scrunched up into the corner, and fell fast asleep.

When he awoke he was shocked to find that their path was ten degrees off course, and he had no idea how long Hugh had been flying in that direction. Clyde was still tired, but he knew it was up to him to get them back on course. Had it been a mistake to choose Hugh to go on this journey with him?

"Hugh, can't you even fly a fixed course?" Clyde shouted. "How long have you been flying with this error?"

"I really don't know," Hugh said. "When did I take over?"

"Okay!" Clyde exclaimed. "That's one strike against you. Let's keep it at that."

Clyde estimated the length of his nap, and then he calculated the heading change required to get back on course. After a fixed amount of time, he estimated he was again on course and returned to the original heading.

After thirty hours, if Clyde's en route correction was right, they hoped they were over land. They found a hole in the cloud layer and descended. Once they were clear of any clouds, they could visually determine that they were in Ireland. Getting better oriented, they flew across St George's Channel before dark and landed in an acceptable farmer's field. The farmer was very hospitable and confirmed that the fliers were in Pembroke Shire, Wales, which meant they were on track. The farmer took them to a local inn so they could have dinner and spend the night there. The local people were always ready to help airplane pilots because they considered meeting them a unique opportunity and an honor.

22

More Delays

Early the next morning, Clyde and Hugh awoke to an offer by a local townsperson to take them to the airplane. They found the airplane just as they left it the night before, so Clyde crawled in and Hugh took his position on the right side of the airplane to wind up the starter. The engine started on the first try, and Hugh crawled in the copilot window and buckled himself in.

"Okay, boss, I'm ready to go," he said.

Clyde opened up the throttle to take off from the farm field. They then turned to a heading for Corydon located just outside of London. Pangborn planned to refuel quickly and be on their way within an hour toward Berlin. As usual, he landed and taxied up to the maintenance hanger area where the fueling equipment was located. Just as he pulled *Miss Veedol* to a halt, the airplane was met by a limousine filled with well-dressed occupants. Almost before the large spinning propeller stopped rotating, the airplane was surrounded by well-wishers. They turned out to be distant relatives of Hugh's.

Mrs. Boardman had apparently cabled them and informed them of the stop-over for fuel. They found this an opportunity for the homecoming of a member of the family, so they all gathered at the airport to greet Hugh. Once there, they insisted that he join them for brunch. Hugh agreed and began to climb into the seat made available for him in the limousine.

"Hugh, what the hell are you doing?" Clyde shouted. "We don't have time for you to go anywhere—I don't care who invited you."

"But these people are family. What do you expect me to do, ignore them?"

Clyde was shocked that Hugh seemed to have no concern for the timeline at all. A leisurely brunch with family he really didn't know was important to him. Was this an indication of how the rest of the flight was going to go? Suddenly Clyde had a sick feeling in the pit of his stomach.

Clyde was noticeably upset. "Have you forgotten that we have a time schedule to meet? Get your damn ass back into the airplane, or I'll leave without you!"

"No, you won't," Hugh said. "We both know that I'm vital to completing the trip."

"Are you trying to screw up the whole record attempt?" Clyde shouted. "You're doing a damn good job, if that's what you want."

"No, that's not what I want. I'll be back sooner than you think," Hugh said.

Clyde watched him get into the limousine and wanted to choke him. The bastard! Clyde thought he should have left Hugh home, but then he realized there would have been no flight without Hugh and his mother's money. Clyde hated being beholden to other people, and that's exactly what he was. He owed Hugh.

Clyde watched the limousine pull away, and off Hugh went with his family, through the gate in the parameter fence. The airplane sat on the ramp with the fuel hose running at full tilt to replace the large amount of fuel burned crossing the Atlantic. Refueling and servicing was done in about thirty minutes, and Clyde was ready to go. He thought, *Hugh, this is strike two—but who is counting but me?*

An hour passed, then two, then six, and Hugh had still not returned. Clyde was furious and began making arrangements to leave alone. Hugh had already caused enough problems by getting them off course, and now they were six hours behind schedule and might never make up the time. He didn't want to see Hugh again and thought he could find his own way home—or anywhere he wanted to go. Clyde didn't give a damn.

He finished the ground check and climbed aboard to have the engine started. Just as the ground crew spun the prop and the engine began to come to life, the limousine pulled up beside the plane and Hugh got out on the far side. Then he began the routine of personally saying good-bye to each member of the family, shaking hands with the men and hugging the women. Five to ten minutes later, while the airplane was still running, he made his way into the cab window and crawled inside.

"Let's go," Hugh said to Clyde.

"You can go, all right. You can go to hell!" Clyde said.

"Maybe if they'd been your family you would have ignored them. But I'm not you," Hugh said.

"Damn it, Hugh, do you realize that you cost us over five hours of time against our record objective? Doesn't that matter to you?"

"We'll make it up somehow," Hugh said.

"No, we won't. Are you part of this effort or not? It may be impossible for us to make up this time. But we're here, so it's time to leave."

"You're too uptight, Clyde," Hugh said. "It's a priority thing. You need to understand that I take care of family and friends before everything else. I haven't seen Aunt May and Uncle Harry since I left England twelve years ago. They are big supporters of my trying to beat the record, so they arranged to meet me here. I think it was important to spend a little time with them, and you should understand that. I can't see that it will have much effect on our overall timing."

Clyde turned away from him and quickly closed up the windows, and almost as quickly, the large WASP engine revved up eagerly in a puff of exhaust.

At 2:30 p.m. they departed England and headed for Berlin's Tempelhof Airport—arriving there in the dark at 7:30 p.m. that evening. After refueling and having a quick meal, they left for Moscow some ten hours behind the Post/Gatty schedule. Clyde tried to control his anger, but he found it very difficult and would barely speak to Hugh.

From Moscow, they flew eastward where they encountered high winds while trying to cross the Ural Mountains. They were buffeted violently while attempting to gain the altitude needed to get over the range. The weather conditions cost more valuable time while they flew perpendicular to the intended flight path.

"This is not good!" the frustrated Clyde shouted. "We're already behind schedule!"

Eventually they found a small pass that allowed them to cross the range. Once on the other side they made an unscheduled stop at Novosibirsk, Russia, to refuel. Clyde kept thinking of how they could recoup the time they'd lost, but he knew that none of the ideas he had would work.

Their next stop was China. All he knew was that he was exhausted and that it was time for him to get some sleep, so Hugh took over the controls once again. When Clyde awoke, Hugh landed at a small village and they were able to find one resident who spoke English. The man informed them that they were not in China as they planned to be, but they were in Mongolia instead. Pangborn glared at Hugh and threw up his arms in disgust. Hugh had obviously lost his way again and gotten completely off course.

23

More Despair

"Do you have any sense of direction at all?" Clyde asked. "I guess you don't even know how to read a compass."

"I wasn't reading a compass. I was reading a map. You shouldn't have slept if you think you could have done better."

In all fairness, navigation was quite difficult as the map-definition was not well-developed, making even dead-reckoning a challenge. A compass heading, along with terrain tracking, was all they had to go by. Further, in bad weather they had to depend on the compass along with time in flight.

While in the clouds, flight instrumentation was almost totally non-existent. In zero visibility conditions, airplane attitude was completely left to the primitive turn and bank indicator, and direction error was indicated by the earth induction compass. Extreme care to avoid icing conditions had to be taken. If severe icing conditions persisted, the only sure survival procedure was to land and wait for better weather.

To recover their planned flight track, they had to travel to their original destination in China and then cover the planned course to Khabarovsk, Siberia—a deviation that caused them to backtrack and lose several more hours of time en route.

Rainy weather persisted throughout the night on their way to Khabarovsk. The storm worsened as they continued until it was nearly impossible to track their position. They had to use side windows to view the ground, as forward vision was completely obscured by the rain striking the windscreen. Wind and turbulence along an apparent squall line made it difficult just to keep control of the airplane.

They knew that they were finally in the area of Khabarovsk. An unimproved airfield was located in the area, but the exact location was not spotted.

Clyde shouted, "Hugh, you will have to watch out for the landing field! It is all that I can do to keep us straight and level!"

It was dark. A few lights were spotted nearby, and the two hoped they indicated the town of Khabarovsk. The airfield was located about one mile east of the town, so Clyde headed in that direction.

"There it is! I see what appears to be the field!" Hugh shouted.

Clyde maneuvered the airplane so that he too could see the location on the ground out the side window. Sure enough, it was directly below but was aligned perpendicular to the prevailing high wind.

"It is going to be a challenge, Hugh, but we have no choice but to try to set it down. It looks like a pile of mud from here. Once I get it on the ground, we'll play hell in keeping it under control. But I'll give it a go!" Clyde hollered.

As he entered final from a sloppy base leg, Clyde yelled, "I guess we had better pray for a *Pangborn Factor* to hold this baby together in this mess!"

Clyde crabbed into the side wind and lowered his upwind wing to slip into what he thought was the runway location. Under the circumstances he did well. The airplane was being tossed both laterally and vertically as the flight path brought them closer and closer to the ground.

Then finally one wheel touched. Clyde attempted to get all wheels down and fought to control *Miss Veedol* against the fierce side wind. About then, the wheels plowed into a puddle formed in the soft clay. The airplane turned, skidded, and ground-looped into a ditch along the strip.

Clyde quickly cut the engine and poked his head out of the pilot's window to survey the situation.

"Well, best thing we can say, Hugh, is that we made it. We have some damage to the gear, but I'm sure we can fix it. The biggest problem might be how we can tow this thing to some place where we can work on it. For now, let's run for it and see if we can get out of the weather."

When they got out of the plane, they were up to their ankles in mud and clay.

Finding an old hanger, they were able to keep themselves dry through the night. In the morning they were greeted by several hundred local curiosity seekers who were willing to tie ropes onto the landing gear and pull the airplane into a sheltered area. There the muddy and somewhat damaged airplane was cleaned and repaired.

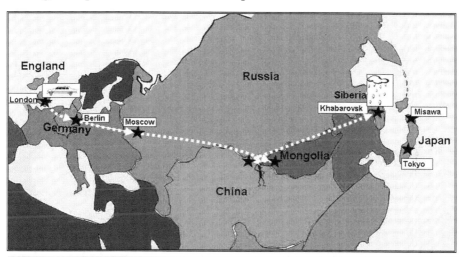

Figure 14. With errors and problems, Miss Veedol worked herself across Europe and Asia to Siberia where she bogged down in a driving rain storm

The people of Khabarovsk were very friendly to the two young aviators and were ready to help in any way they could. One of the locals who spoke some English offered to let them stay at his home and provide them with food while they were delayed in town.

"From all indications the bad weather is here to stay for a while," their host said in broken English.

Clyde and Hugh just looked at each other.

"I know this must be disappointing for both of you," the man said. "My guess is that you will not be able to leave for several days."

Already twenty-seven hours behind the time schedule set by Post and Gatty, Clyde and Hugh were noticeably disgusted and resigned to abandoning the goal they had set out to meet. They both knew that any possibility of breaking the around-the-world record was hopeless. At least they were safe, being taken care of, and in a good position to plan their next move.

24

A Change in Plans

The rain persisted over the next couple of days, and Clyde grew more disgusted as he watched his dream of breaking the around-the-world record disappear. Meanwhile, he continued to think about their current situation and tried to derive the best plan to follow from there. Hugh spent the time playing cards with their host. And as he watched them, Clyde wished he could be more like Hugh.

"In some ways, I wish that Mary Ellen was here and in other ways, I am glad that she is not," Hugh remarked. "I'd like her here just to keep me company but I'd hate for her to be here just to follow me around like a 'puppy dog'. Besides, look at our living conditions, this place is just like a 'shit hole'. Can you imagine Mary Ellen –or mother living in a place like this! We accept it because we have to, but we certainly aren't living 'high on the hog.'"

Then, one day, Clyde ended the card playing. *Miss Veedol* was stuck in Siberia, and they had a long trip just to get home. So it was time for both, Clyde and Hugh, to prepare the airplane for their journey back halfway around the world. Hugh had already said that he, instead, would rather continue playing cards.

"Who won?" Clyde asked.

"He did," Hugh replied as he pointed to the man on his left. "He took me for a couple hundred bucks!"

"Shit," Clyde said. "And you wanted to keep playing? That's nuts."

"It's a good way to pass the time—better than staring out the window at the rain. Besides, I could have won it back from him."

"Maybe you'll get a chance to do that later," Clyde said.

At the end of the day, one of the residents offered them the use of his small cottage that was within walking distance, and they decided to accept the offer. The cottage had a wood heating and cooking stove and they were able to warm up and cook dinner from the supplies given them by the locals. They took turns cooking and cleaning before crawling into their bunks for the night. Evenings were spent discussing plans for the next day as well as other possibilities for their return trip to the United States.

"We really couldn't control what happened, even if we wanted to," Clyde said to Hugh.

"I thought you blamed the fact that I had lunch with my family," Hugh said.

"Well it didn't help unless we might have beaten this squall—but in the end I suspect it had no effect..." Clyde said.

"I don't understand," Hugh said. "What do you mean?"

Clyde laughed. "What I mean is that it had no effect on the weather. It did put us way behind schedule, but I was hoping we'd be able to catch up."

"I guess I never thought we would," Hugh said.

"Well, it could be a lot worse," Clyde explained, "We are at least in good shape, and so is our transportation. Only our objective has been shattered."

"It turns out that those so-called delays that I caused, you know, the ones that got you so upset, didn't matter anyway, right?" Hugh said. "That's the way things go. There is really no reason to bust your tail, as other more significant events will ultimately control everything."

"No, you're wrong!" Clyde insisted. "To make any significant achievement, you have to do your best. There is no other way. Then if anything happens, it happens. But you must always work hard and do your part."

They wired the Around-The-World Corporation for advice or any new information regarding other events they might want to attempt. They heard back that they would qualify for Japan's *Asahi Shim bun* newspaper's twenty-five thousand dollar prize for being the first nonstop crossing of the Pacific Ocean. Of course, this was something Clyde had already been thinking about, and he grew excited that the opportunity was right there in front of them. Suddenly, the round-the-world record lost its significance.

Clyde turned to Hugh in an excited manner. "Since we have to return to the U.S., anyway, why don't we do it for the glory?" he asked.

"Are you only in this for the glory?" Hugh wondered out loud.

"Sure, why are we setting way out here in Siberia in the first place? We were trying to set one record and, unfortunately, we failed. We shouldn't stop here, let's go after another and more impressive record. We can do it!" If there was a soap box, Clyde would have been on it. His arms were waving and his voice shouting at times to get Hugh impressed with the idea. "*Miss Veedol* can be modified to help us cross the Pacific Ocean nonstop and collect that prize money.

Hugh being scared of the idea said, "You've got to be out of your mind, Clyde. I know of six earlier attempts, and they all ended in disaster. Three good pilots lost their lives attempting to do the same thing you want to do. I have a lot of respect for *Miss Veedol*, but she is far from being capable of such a feat. Just think about it, it's two thousand miles further than what Lindbergh flew in the Ryan NYP."

"Hey, this is the 1930's, not the 1920's. We are on the brink of world history, man. *Miss Veedol* is probably the best airplane ever built," Clyde said as he pointed out the window towards the airplane parked just outside. "If any airplane can make it, she can. We both know her limitations."

"Hugh, you know we have to extend the range by a considerable margin. We can start by completely loading her full of fuel—and then determine if she can carry all that added weight or for that matter, take off with it. We'll have to work together on it, but I know it is possible. Are you in?"

"Okay I guess you're right," Hugh said. "It will be a challenge, but this is best time to consider it."

* * * * *

With Clyde's encouragement and his good knowledge of airplane modification, the two set out to develop a plan. Clyde knew that Hugh was grateful for Clyde's knowledge, because this was something Hugh would never be able to accomplish on his own.

"Whatever changes we have to make to *Miss Veedol*, the first thing we need to do is go to Japan and establish a place to launch the flight."

Hugh nodded. "Do you have any idea of where that might be?"

92

"Earlier attempts have left from Sabishiro Beach near Misawa about two hundred miles north of Tokyo—but I don't know about that for sure," Clyde said.

"What do we need to do now?" Hugh asked.

"First, we have to cable the Around-the-World Corporation tomorrow morning and ask them to contact the U.S. Embassy in Japan. The embassy will need to contact the Japanese Aviation Bureau and get permission for us to fly across and land in Japan. Once we get that approval and the weather improves, we have to be ready to depart for Tachikawa airport in Tokyo immediately."

Clyde began to seriously study the possible changes that could be made to the Bellanca to extend the range to make the fifty-five-hundred-mile trip across the Pacific.

"I've thought about this for a long time and I know that we will have to add as much fuel to *Miss Veedol* as we can," Clyde said. "The large wing is already half full, and it is in the right location to supply the engine using gravity feed. The seven-hundred-gallon capacity built into the airplane at the factory is impressive, but it is far from being adequate for achieving the range needed.

There was a rudimentary world map hanging on the wall that Clyde and Hugh hung there. Clyde kept staring at it and using it to make points with Hugh.

"The only space not being used is in the cab beside the existing large auxiliary tank and in the aft cabin," Hugh said.

"That is mostly correct," Clyde added. "In addition, it might be possible to locate say maybe thirty-five gallons in the area outside ahead of the belly tank—in the chin area." Clyde animated the lower airplane contour as he spoke. "That would require us to build some sort of a fairing around it to save drag. All of these locations would need to be hooked up to the same old manual wobble pump to supply the fuel to the main wing tanks."

Clyde sat forward and began to write out notes as he talked and planned. "The extra tanks can be located behind the aerodynamic center of the wing, giving us some improvement in cruise performance if done correctly." He drew a simple Teeter-totter stick diagram on the pad between them to simplify the balance issues. "As we burn that fuel off, we may have to give some special consideration to loading to regain elevator control power for landing."

"There is room in the cab area for a fairly large tank. But how much can we add before we exceed the structural strength limitation of the wing and body?" Hugh asked.

"No one knows the answer to that question, Hugh. We know that certain margins were used to design the structure. We'll have to assume those margins are real and do our planning around that. If we add one hundred thirty gallons, that would probably add fifteen hundred pounds total for the fuel, tank, and plumbing," Clyde said. Clyde was scribbling on a paper between him and Hugh while talking.

"I suppose we can consider carrying some fuel in small tins as well if we can devise a way of transferring the fuel to the upper tanks. That coupled—"

"Wait a minute Clyde, wait a minute. Stop, stop you can't keep adding weight on like that," cried Hugh. "There has to be a limit!"

"Let me finish, you have to start somewhere. That coupled with the thirty-five gallons in the chin area of the structure may be about all we can take on. I figure with all of these changes, the allowable maximum weight for the aircraft will be exceeded by about three thousand pounds.

"Wow, that isn't possible, is it?" asked Hugh.

"Well, we do know this, that'll bring the takeoff gross weight considerably higher than the structure was designed for or ever tested for by Bellanca on this airplane," Clyde said. "We'll have to assume that the structure is strong enough to support the load if we have the performance to get it off the ground with that high of a wing loading."

"Will that amount of fuel get us there?" Hugh asked.

"It might," Clyde said. "But only under ideal conditions—that means no margin for error, adverse winds, or reserves—to assure success we need everything to go perfectly."

Hugh sat back in his chair and lit a cigarette.

"Do you have to do that?" Clyde asked.

"When I'm feeling stressed, I do."

"Try to do it when I'm not around," Clyde said.

Hugh angrily snapped back, "This happens to be something I enjoy, it isn't expensive, and no one has proved that it is harmful to anyone. So get off of my case! I only wished that we were both smokers so that you wouldn't be bugging me all the time."

"Well, as a non-smoker, I don't enjoy it," Clyde responded. "I would think that you would see what it causes to you as a flyer. Anyway, let's get back to our Pacific problem."

"Here's something else we might consider," Clyde said, thinking out loud. "Back in 1919, a scheme was devised by an Australian named Harry Hawker where he jettisoned the landing gear to save weight. It would also be a significant drag reduction. I made some calculation last night that suggested that the drag reduction we would realize could increase our speed by up to fifteen miles per hour—on a forty-hour flight that's six hundred miles—that would do it! In addition we'll reduce our weight by three hundred pounds."

Hugh reached for another cigarette. "You're kidding me, Clyde, aren't you? Land without landing gear? It was added to the airplane for a reason. We'll need to land the thing sometime—how will we do that without landing gear?"

"We'll cross that issue when we come to it," Clyde said.

Hugh took a few drags on the cigarette, "Sure, after we crash."

"There is that risk. Sure, it will be tricky, but I think it's possible. Right now that option gives us an airplane that should make the range. Maybe for landing we can add some sort of skid plates to the belly to protect us for a single landing. That would cost us some weight, but I expect they wouldn't cost us too much."

Hugh got up and began to pace around the room. Clyde wished he could say something that would calm Hugh's nerves. Clyde saw his plan as a solution, but with risks, while Hugh was definitely concerned about the idea. It was obvious that Hugh thought that anyone proposing such an idea must be out of their mind.

In trying to calm Hugh down, Clyde asked him to think of the airplane as a sled. "If we killed the engine at the last moment so the propeller stopped to rest horizontally, we could skid the plane quite well on sandy soil. We'd be at zero fuel so that the gross weight would be low, and the chance of fire would be small if we dump all of the fuel. Our stall or approach speed will be at a snail's pace," Clyde assured him. "I'm sure we can do it with no problem."

Way down deep inside, the idea didn't rest well with Clyde either. The problem was that he couldn't come up with any other option. A crash landing at the end of their mission wasn't the way to enter the world of glory. But he had to stretch the airplane's performance for everything it had, and he felt as though he was forced into this option.

"Hugh, I know those are pretty extensive modifications," Clyde said. "We'll have to get started on them right after we get to Japan. There we'll have the means to design, fabricate, and install all of these new systems."

Hugh shook his head. "Well, I guess I'm in. I hope you're right, and I hope you know what you're doing. Otherwise..."

Clyde slapped him on the back. "Think positively." He continued, "I believe we can remove the bolts that hold the gear and the airplane together, then drill and pin the gear onto the airplane along with springs to help unjoin the joints. Cables attached to the pins could be lead to the pilot's station. When the time is right, the pilot can pull on the cable to release the gear."

"What about the Japanese?" Hugh asked. "How do you think they'll feel about all these modifications?"

"We'll have to keep anything we do regarding the landing gear a secret from the Japanese. There have been so many airplane failures recently in these record-breaking attempts that they have taken the responsibility to approve the airworthiness of every airplane leaving their country. I'm sure that the Japanese Aviation Bureau would not think very highly of a system to drop our landing gear."

25

Let's Make a Run for It

Two days later they still had not received word from the U.S. Embassy, but a brief break in the weather front occurred in the area. The rain stopped momentarily, and a sandy part of the runway surface began to harden enough to support the airplane. There was a definite threat of the rain starting again soon. The two considered that the Japanese approval they were waiting for was primarily a formality, and with that in mind they decided to make a run for it and depart the partially dry Siberian field and head for Japan. So they said good-bye to their gracious hosts, jumped into the airplane, and departed.

After several hours of flight, the darkened skies cleared, and the whole countryside burst open in the sunshine ahead of them. The scene, with its green forests and farmlands in the foreground framed by towering mountains, was a beautiful sight to both of them.

Figure 15. Making a run for their departure from Siberia to Japan

"Look at that ocean," Hugh said. "Have you ever seen anything so blue? Look at the white line where the blue sea meets the shoreline."

They were both thrilled because they could already visualize the second part of their two-part adventure taking shape. To record the beautiful scene and to verify the route taken, they decided to take a large number of photographs using the cameras they had with them, taking 35mm stills and 16mm movies.

It was a full-time job for one of them to take pictures while the other piloted the airplane toward the Japanese landing site. Little did they know that they were flying over military-restricted airspace and taking pictures of sensitive Japanese facilities.

During that time they received a radio message defining directions to the Tachikawa airport relative to Tokyo and telling them that "the landing approval was being sought." Following the new directions, they spotted the airport dead ahead. Clyde approached, landed, and taxied to an area that appeared to have a great deal of activity.

"I guess the word got around announcing our arrival," Clyde said. "We seem to be getting a better reception here that at any other stop throughout our trip."

Hugh smiled. "It looks like they even brought out the top brass. I wouldn't have thought they'd be so happy to see us."

They parked the airplane and went through the procedural shutdown. Then the two, weary from their flight, exited the cab window and dropped onto the ground. Their first greeter rushed up to Clyde and demanded to see his landing papers. When he admitted he didn't have any, he and Hugh were immediately arrested and taken to the local police headquarters.

At the headquarters, Clyde was taken out of the holding and into a separate room down the hall. Several uniformed officials followed him in before they shut the door. It was more than an hour before he was returned to rejoin his flying companion.

"What's going on?" Hugh asked once they were alone again.

"We jumped the gun," Clyde said. "We should have waited in Siberia for the flight plan approval. I don't know if they would have given us a detailed enough plan to skirt around certain areas or warned us about taking pictures, but for now they have us on three counts of treason: flying into their airspace without approval, landing in their country without approval, and taking pictures of all of the military establishments along the way."

In Japan at that time, the military had almost complete control over the government. Most significant offices, including the office of Prime Minister, were filled by the military. When Chinese nationalists began to seriously challenge Japan about a conflict with China, the Japanese armed forces earlier in that year moved to occupy Manchuria. Within a year, the Japanese Air Force actually bombarded Shanghai in order to protect Japanese residents from anti-Japanese movements in China. Thus, tensions in the country were high at the time when *Miss Veedol* flew in unannounced.

Clyde and Hugh were both placed under house arrest and told that they would be staying at the Imperial Hotel in Tokyo. They weren't locked up, but their travels beyond their rooms in the hotel were strictly monitored. *Miss Veedol* was locked up in an abandoned hanger at the airport and was off-limits to them.

26

At the Bellanca Factory

Joe Ruggerio was racing to work at the Bellanca Airplane Company in Wilmington, Delaware. He knew that he would be expected to know all the latest on *Miss Veedol* so he could make a report to Giuseppe Bellanca the first thing that morning. The latest thing that he heard late the night before is that the *Miss Veedol* had landed in Tokyo and the two fliers had been arrested.

He had already told Giuseppe that the flight had been plagued with problems. They lost time crossing the Atlantic; they lost time in London; and then, of all things, they got lost on their way to China. The worst thing was the muddy landing in Siberia. He called the New York office and found out that the reason they were in Japan was to attempt to cross the Pacific Ocean. *The guys must be nuts!* he thought.

The day earlier, he had his engineers look at that option. And the engineers decided the whole equation blew up when they attempted to get much range out of the airplane. The engineers said that over one thousand gallons of fuel would be required—and they couldn't suggest where it could be stored. They already loaded the airplane up as much as they thought was possible. And it was not only full, but by their calculations the airplane would become so heavy that it couldn't take off.

And then there were other things: Where would they try to take off from? What kind of weather could they expect—or run into? How much emergency equipment would be needed for a crossing—the Pacific is a big place! How could they stay warm and efficient for such a long flight?

100

Maybe it was best that they got arrested, Joe thought. *It could possibly save both of their lives.*

He arrived at his office and immediately got on the phone to *Miss Veedol's* New York office. There they were not too optimistic. The Japanese government was military run, and the people they talked to were not too friendly. Pangborn and Herndon were being held for treason—a very serious offence in Japan at that time. The airplane was not available to them, so any modifications required to attempt the trans-Pacific flight were completely out of the question.

As he was still on the phone, Giuseppe walked in and sat down at Joe's conference table. He could only hear one side of the conversation, but he knew Joe was on the phone talking about his number-one item of interest, so he didn't interrupt. The whole world was watching these guys trying to accomplish great things using an airplane his company had built.

Soon, Joe got off the phone and with a long face began explaining the situation as he knew it to Giuseppe.

"I don't know what their chances are in getting freed. But if they do, maybe it would be in our best interests to send one of our top men over there to discourage them in attempting such a hair-brained flight. This guy Clyde Pangborn suggested exceeding the airplane design limits and referred to them as using the 'Pangborn Factor.' But I don't think he understands airplane design as well as our own design team. He impressed me as being a smart, solid thinker, but still…"

Giuseppe thought out loud—"If they attempt such a crossing and fail using one of our best airplanes, what would be the consequences?"

Joe explained, "When we built that particular airplane we used extra caution. All of the structural wood was hand-selected to assure it at least measured up to being above the weak wood samples. Still, the specified maximum takeoff gross weight is six thousand pounds." Joe threw both of his hands to his head and raised them as though he was to pull his head from it's sockets. His hair was thrown out of it normal neat arrangement. "Theoretically the wings can break off if they hit a limit gust or severe bump in the runway by operating fifty percent above that limitation. We can only pray that they don't try something dumb!"

"They installed the larger WASP 425 engine on *Miss Veedol,* which will help get a larger load into the air if the wings can hold up. I wish there were some way of adjusting the propeller pitch during the flight to optimize it for any condition. They might be able to get off of the ground, but they maybe will have problems staying in the air as the speed increases.

"I guess, Mr. Bellanca, that we can only wait and keep a keen eye on what is happening over there. We can only hope and pray that Clyde Pangborn knows what he is doing. I suspect that his sidekick—err—aw—Hugh—Hugh Herndon can't be of much help."

27

Under House Arrest

In the Imperial Hotel, Clyde and Hugh were given adjacent rooms on the first floor. Two military guards were stationed just outside their rooms in the hallway. Other hotel guests who saw the armed guards wondered why the guards were there and felt they were disruptive. Otherwise, the hall was empty aside from the wall tables filled with freshly cut flowers. The hotel designed by Frank Lloyd Wright was well-appointed and typically frequented only by the well-to-do.

The rooms were not at all like a jail. They were roomy and well-decorated with a bathroom that included a shower stall and hot running water. They were fundamentally four-sided rooms with the door wall adjoining the hallway and the outside wall containing a vertically sliding window. The window faced a well-groomed garden area with some sort of shrubbery at the back of the garden. Being on the ground floor, the window sills in their rooms were only about four feet from the ground level outdoors.

Inside, besides a comfortable bed, the rooms were furnished with a divan, an overstuffed chair, and a table and two chairs. There were no books or magazines or any other way to pass the time. There were pencils and paper, however, which were useful to Clyde for doing design work. Although Clyde and Hugh were confined, the accommodations permitted them an opportunity to shower and clean up—something that they had been unable to do for over a week by this time.

Clyde and Hugh quickly learned that they could communicate through the wall without shouting. The building was constructed using single-studded walls with little care for muffling any stray noise. By placing their ears in glass tumblers held tightly to the wall, the sound vibrations allowed them to hear each other.

"This is pretty plush for a prison, don't you think?" Clyde asked Hugh.

Hugh laughed. "It's not bad. Though I ordered lobster and they didn't even laugh."

"It's Japan, remember?" Clyde said. "Maybe they don't have lobster."

"Oh, they have it, all right. They just don't want to serve it to a con like me."

"They should bring dinner soon, so we'll see if you get your lobster," Clyde said. "In the meantime, we can relax in style. Better yet, we can probably slip out at night and see some of the sights."

"Now that sounds like a good plan," Hugh said.

A few hours later, there was a slight knock on Clyde's door, and a beautiful, slim, Japanese lady in her late twenties entered with a tray full of food and drinks. Clyde didn't pay much attention to the food, but he thought the service was way beyond what he would have expected for a prisoner. The attendant wasn't dressed like most Japanese women in a flowing tight dress; she was wearing military style fatigues.

"I'm Yumiko," she said. "I'll be your food server during your stay here."

In perfect English, she added, "It's such a thrill to meet you. I have always been intrigued by pilots and airplanes, especially people like you who are trying to accomplish great things with them. We live in very exciting times, don't we?"

"I'm very pleased to meet you, Yumiko, And I must say, you're right, we do live in exciting times." He extended his hand to her. "My name is Clyde Pangborn, and I'm a pilot."

"Yes, I know who you are. My father was very interested in knowing about your plans because he has a manufacturing business that makes parts for some of the local businesses that build airplanes."

"If I wasn't in this predicament, I would certainly want to meet him," Clyde said as Yumiko headed for the door. "You speak almost perfect English without a hint of an accent. Why is that?"

Yumiko smiled at him. "I went to school in your country for four years," she said. "I got a degree in dietetics at the University of Washington. I learned how to feed large groups of people, but I never thought those people would be prisoners under house arrest."

"I'm sure you didn't."

"I have to tend to your partner next door. It was a thrill to meet you, Mr. Clyde."

After she closed the door, Clyde quickly placed the glass on the wall adjoining Hugh's room to listen. She had much the same conversation as she had with him, except that she asked numerous questions about, "the pilot next door, Mr. Clyde."

That evening Hugh and Clyde were both exhausted and spent the night in their rooms. They found the beds very comfortable, and when they lay down they both fell asleep. Because of the hectic schedule they'd both become accustomed to during the last few months, they both awoke the next morning long before the sun rose. Clyde spent some time surveying the surroundings to see what else it might offer. In doing so, he discovered that the windows weren't locked and that he could reach the ground outside with little difficulty. Just as a trial, he slipped outside and knocked on Hugh's window. Within seconds, Hugh was standing there looking at him.

Hugh opened the window. "What the hell are you doing? What do you think they would do if they saw you outside your room?"

"I don't know. But this is pretty convenient, don't you think? Come on out and we'll go and visit our bird."

"No way," Hugh said. "Yumiko will be coming with breakfast soon, and we'd better not get caught. We might wind up in a prison a lot less comfortable than this one."

Just as Clyde climbed back into his room and closed the window, he heard a soft knock on the door. He opened it and saw Yumiko standing there holding a tray of food with a beautiful red rose lying on top.

"What might I ask is the occasion?" Clyde asked, not being able to stop from smiling.

"I just thought I'd bring you a gift to brighten your day," she said. "I hope your enjoy your breakfast. Is there anything else I can do for you?"

"No," Clyde said. "Thank you. Maybe if you have any spare time you can stop by and we can talk for a while. I'd be very interested in learning about your father's business, since it's about airplanes."

"They keep me pretty busy during working hours, but maybe I can stop by after work sometime," she said.

Clyde was quite excited to learn more about airplane fabrication and see Yumiko later, so after he finished breakfast he showered, put on some clean clothes, and combed his hair. While he was doing this he thought of Diane and felt a pang of guilt about Yumiko. This wasn't the first time in his life he'd been involved with two women at the same time, but he knew Diane was different and was as attracted to her as he was to Yumiko. Well, he wasn't with Diane now. He was with Yumiko. And for now, he wanted to get to know her better.

He saw Yumiko again at lunchtime and then at dinner. Each time she was very friendly and pleasant. He began to show considerable interest in her. At dinner they had a cup of coffee together, and he shared his peach cobbler with her.

"This is delicious," Clyde said. "Thank the chef for me."

Yumiko rose to her feet. "I'd better go. Maybe I'll see you later." She then opened the door and closed it behind her.

Later than evening, Clyde heard a light knock at his door. When he opened it, he was only a little surprised to see Yumiko standing there.

"May I come in?" she asked.

"Of course. I'm glad to see you again. How was your day?"

She stepped in, and he closed the door behind her.

"It was long, and I'm glad it's over," she said. "I could hardly wait for the day to end, but it went by very slowly. I wanted the chance to spend more time with you and find out more about your plans."

Clyde explained the around-the-world trip and what had gone wrong, and she was sympathetic. He also told her how they happened to be in Tokyo and their current situation.

"Right now we need to make some modifications to the airplane so that it's ready if we get a chance to make the attempt to cross the Pacific."

"Do you even have access to the airplane?" Yumiko asked.

"Not really. They have it locked up in a hanger at the airport. We could do the work at night if they would let us go there on occasion. With the current arrangement, I can't see any opportunity to ready the bird. Maybe we should just slip out the window while no one is watching."

"That's pretty risky," Yumiko replied. "If they ever catch you leaving your room without an escort, they would put you in a hard cell."

Clyde frowned. "We really need to work on the airplane, or our plans to cross the Pacific aren't possible. Would you feel responsible for notifying the authorities if you knew we tried that?"

"No, not as long as they can't tie me to anything," she said. "I don't see how you can get anything accomplished when you don't have any tools or other material you need."

"Don't worry about that," Clyde said.

"Maybe I can help. I'll check with my father and see if he's willing to support your dreams."

"Thanks, Yumiko. I hope you can be trusted. Maybe you can give me some idea of what you find out tomorrow."

"You can trust me. Just make sure you don't associate with me if you ever get caught."

"I hope they never catch me," Clyde said. "But I assure you that your name is safe."

Yumiko backed out of the door and closed it behind her. She didn't say anything to Hugh about the plan, so Clyde talked to him through the wall and brought him up to speed. Hugh was obviously nervous about the scheme, but he couldn't come up with any other way to get the job done.

The two men slept well but again woke early the next morning. This time Clyde slipped out the window and was successful in getting Hugh to join him outside. They found that the shrubbery at the back of their yard, within ten feet of their back window, was part of an arboretum. Within the arboretum was a hiking trail leading toward the outskirts of town and the airport. They later learned that the trail passed *Miss Veedol's* hangar, which was located in the airport perimeter adjacent to town. The trail could give them a means of travel in darkness between their hotel and the airplane.

Later in the morning, Yumiko arrived with the breakfast tray. She had good news for him. "Both father and I would be willing to meet with you at night if you are serious about escaping and working on your airplane. It will be risky for all of us, and we must have a good plan to avoid being caught and identified. When do you think we should try it?"

"We have to move, and we have to move fast," Clyde said. "How about meeting at eleven o'clock tonight at the hangar? If you have any flashlights, you might want to bring them. They may be the only means we'll have to see what we're doing. Is that doable for you?"

"Yes," she said. "We'll be there at eleven somewhere on the side where there is less chance that anyone will notice us. The door there is secured by a key-operated padlock. How will we get in? The place is constructed of corrugated steel."

"I don't know yet," Clyde answered. "We'll have to take a look at the situation first before the problem can be addressed."

"Do you think it will be difficult?" Yumiko asked.

"If it is, we'll overcome it." He smiled at her, and she smiled back at him. "Don't worry."

Clyde gave Yumiko a big hug—lasting longer than the typical good-bye between friends. She whispered softly in his ear, "Please be careful and good luck."

He nodded. "I will, and you be careful too."

She slipped out the door.

28

Modifying Miss Veedol

That night around 10:00 p.m., after the lights were turned off, the two Americans slipped out of their windows and onto the vegetation-shrouded trail behind the hotel complex. They hustled in the dark, having only the moonlight to guide their way. At times they had problems staying centered on the trail.

Clyde laughed when Hugh weaved toward the right. "You're walking like you've had a few too many. Watch it or you might wind up in God-knows-where."

"I'm fine, what's with you and Yumiko?"

Clyde turned away. "Nothing, we're friends. She spends as much time with you."

"Not really. And her face doesn't light up when she looks at me. She's got a thing for you, buddy boy, and I think you like her too. What are you going to do about Diane?"

"If I could get hold of a phone I'd call her, but there's no way. Maybe Yumiko…"

"Oh, so you're going to ask one of your girlfriends to get you a phone so you can call your other girlfriend. Real smart, Clyde, real smart."

Clyde shook his head. "Neither one of them is my girlfriend. We need to hurry."

Hugh looked at him out of the corner of his eye and grinned.

Their 11:00 p.m. deadline was rapidly approaching. Five minutes before the appointed hour, they reached the hanger. No one could be seen in the darkness behind the hanger. Suddenly they heard a faint whisper.

"*Is that you, Clyde?*"

Two people could only be seen outlined in the darkness. Under the circumstances, Clyde and Hugh could only surmise that it was Yumiko and her father. Hugh peeked at Clyde, and Clyde put his finger to his lips.

"Yes, we made it. Are we on time?"

At that moment a flashlight came on.

"Shroud that with your hand as best you can so the light will be hard to see from a distance," Clyde said.

A short time was spent greeting each other and making a brief introduction to Yumiko's father, Yosh. Clyde and Hugh liked him right away and thought he was intelligent and quite knowledgeable about airplanes. He also seemed to be quite overprotective of Yumiko and kept his arm around her waist the whole time they were talking. Clyde had no problem understanding his position. He had no way of knowing how much Yumiko had told her father about him.

"I told Daddy about you, and he said he would like to help you out with your ambitious plans," Yumiko said.

"We really appreciate what you're doing," Clyde said to Yosh, and he nodded. Clyde wondered how good Yosh's English was.

"How do we get in?" Hugh asked.

"I don't know how we do that," Yumiko said. "We looked the place over, and it seems to be fairly well locked up."

Just then Hugh spoke up. "Don't worry. I haven't seen a lock yet that I couldn't pick."

"Why haven't you said anything until now?" Clyde said.

"I enjoy seeing you worry."

Clyde stared at Hugh in amazement. "Why do you know so much about picking locks, for God's sake?"

"In my earlier days, it was the only way I had to see some of my friends who were being protected by their parents," Hugh replied.

Clyde didn't understand what Hugh meant, but he decided not to pursue it any further. "Well, let's not discuss that anymore," he said. "Can you get into this place, Hugh?"

"Piece of cake," Hugh said. In less than thirty seconds, he had the backdoor open.

"Wow, that's one big airplane," Yosh said. "Is that what it takes to cross the Pacific?"

"We think it's the right bird, but we still need to make significant changes to it," Clyde said. "To save weight and drag, we need to install removable pins in the landing gear so that it can be jettisoned after take-off. In addition we need to install a large one-hundred-thirty-gallon fuel tank on the floor and a thirty-five-gallon tank in the chin with fairing. We need to also add more oil capacity, as the engine is expected to run nonstop for possibly over forty hours. Is there any way you can help us accomplish these changes? We don't know how much time we have, but we have to be ready to go at almost any time. To be safe, we have to plan on having everything finished in a month."

"I think I can help you," Yosh said. "I have all the tools you will need to make any kind of modification, but they are all electric and located at my shop two miles from here. Maybe we can fabricate the modifications there and assemble them here at night."

They then made arrangements to meet at the hangar at 11:00 p.m. each night. The lock on the side door would be "farmer locked". That is, it would be aligned to make it appear that it was closed, but in reality it was always open.

29

The Verdict Is Released

As the modification process progressed, Yosh proved to be very competent and quickly helped develop the specifications needed to make the changes. He realized that his livelihood was in great jeopardy if he was caught helping the prisoners. But because he was doing something that he loved, it was worth it to him to support the adventurers.

Each night, Clyde and Hugh would sneak out at 10:00 p.m., arrive at the hanger at 11:00, where they met Yumiko and Yosh, and work until 4:00 a.m. There just didn't seem to be enough time to get it all done. Both Clyde and Yumiko wanted to have more time together but couldn't figure out how to fit it into an already full schedule.

Figure 16. Night time modification to Miss Veedol

On the fourth day, the team had just assembled and was hard at work around 11:30 p.m. when they heard a strange commotion outside of the front door.

"It is the police checking the security," whispered Yosh. "Turn off the lights and work your way toward the storeroom in the aft."

In the darkness, the four were already familiar with the hanger interior as they had learned to work in near darkness for several days already. Clyde held Yumiko's hand and led her around and over the numerous obstacles in the large hanger. Once they reached the storeroom, the four snuggled inside and quietly pulled the door closed.

About six security police entered the hanger and turned on the lights. They noticed what might be signs of activity around the plane and commented to each other about it. The security team continued the search of the hangar but luckily did not open the door to the storeroom. When they turned off the light and exited the building, Yosh overheard one say that they had better go back to the hotel and make sure that the prisoners were still in their rooms.

When clear, Clyde and Hugh exited the side door in a rush and began to run for the hotel. Yosh and Yumiko took their time to gather up any identifying tools, pack them up, and carry them to their automobile parked several blocks away. They then headed for home, worried about the outcome of the two Americans.

Meanwhile, Clyde and Hugh ran down the dark trail toward their rooms. Luckily, there was a full moon, bright enough to cast shadows. It made it possible for the two to run fairly fast. Although they were fairly young, they were not in the best of shape. When they arrived at their hotel, they slid open their windows and crawled inside. Clyde got into the room just when two security guards burst in.

"Have you been here all evening?" one of them asked.

"Well, of course," answered Clyde. "I normally stay up late to exercise so that I can stay healthy while under confinement."

They noted his disheveled and sweaty appearance and his labored breathing.

"Okay," one of them said as they started to leave the room. "Have a good night."

The guards also checked Hugh's room, but he was able to jump into bed before they opened the door.

After that close call the team considered new ways of operating. Instead of all working inside the hanger at the same time, one of them was always stationed near the front of the hangar on the lookout for any arriving vehicles. As it turned out, the lookout wasn't needed, as an inspection never occurred again after that one time.

Clyde and Yumiko still wanted to have more time together. During lunch, Clyde suggested to Yumiko that he would leave the hotel at 9:00 p.m. and arrive at the hanger by 10:00 p.m. She was ecstatic about the plan and assured him that she would be there early.

At 10:00 p.m. the next day, Clyde arrived at the hanger, meeting Yumiko by the door.

They embraced as though they hadn't seen each other for a year. Yumiko told Clyde, "I never dreamed I'd ever have these feelings toward an American."

"My feelings for you get stronger every day in spite of the obstacles we're dealing with." Clyde said then paused and looked into her eyes. "I have to tell you that I'm also involved with a girl back home. Her name is Diane, a nurse at one of the hospitals there."

"You have feelings for her," Yumiko said.

"I do. I have to be honest with you."

They continued to talk and exchange stories of their lives and family, likes and dislikes. To them it seemed like only seconds before the hour was over and Hugh and Yosh arrived.

Three weeks passed, and the modifications were taking shape. Clyde would determine the type of modification that was needed and design the changes as well as make sketches and slip them to Yosh. Yosh would have the changes laid out in detail and return the drawings to Clyde for review.

Some of the parts were fairly large and intricate. Yosh would have them fabricated in his machine shops and disguise them from his workers as being miscellaneous parts for a secret project that only he had the need to know. All of the parts were fit-checked but transported to the hanger disassembled.

The landing gear was disassembled in the hanger. To do this, the airplane had to be supported in such a way that it wasn't obvious. All four of them continued to fear that someone might someday want to make an inspection of the hanger contents. Landing gear parts were quickly taken to Yosh's shop, modified, returned, and put in place on the airplane so that it always looked whole. A great deal of the work would have been impossible had Yosh not provided the support.

The large tank mounted in the cab was assembled. But they were unable to perform a leak check because they had not yet devised the means of loading such a large amount of liquid in the secret chambers.

* * * * *

The relationship between Clyde and Yumiko was maturing. Clyde knew that the day would come when he would either be sentenced to a very long stay in a hard cell on Japanese soil or be released to continue his daring flight to the United States. Both options would be an end to his relationship with Yumiko. Further, he felt guilty for his feelings about her when he already had a ripening relationship with Diane in Boise. Even though he had explained his relationship with Diane to Yumiko in hopes of cooling her infatuation, he felt her fascination with him as a somewhat famous flyboy, was overwhelming to her. He had never dreamed that pursuing help in making modifications to the airplane would lead to a romantic dilemma.

During the day, Yumiko fed some of the officials trying the espionage case against Clyde and Hugh. From time to time she would over hear the status and pass it onto Clyde to keep him aware of what she found out. Recently she learned that the Japanese officials agreed that their picture-taking was not done maliciously. But the photography of sensitive areas was still a serious infraction. The Japanese did not want to let the two prisoners walk off scot-free, and they wanted to make an example out of the case. They might decree a sentence at any time.

Hugh, Clyde, Yosh, and Yumiko all felt the pressure of timing. Hopefully Clyde and Hugh and their airplane would be released. If that happened, they would have to be ready to go immediately before the Japanese changed their minds.

After five weeks, Yumiko delivered dinner to Hugh first and then brought Clyde his dinner. Instead of leaving after work she returned to Clyde's room.

"I'd like to stay here and sneak out of the window with you tonight at ten. I think you need the extra hour to work on the airplane."

Clyde understood what she really wanted as he felt the same way. Instead of responding with any talk of the airplane, he reached for her, took her in his arms, and passionately kissed her on her neck. She closed her eyes, raised her chin, and snuggled her face in his neck. Their embrace tightened as their lips found each other. They made their way to his bed as he turned out the lights.

Hours later they arose and prepared to escape out the window. Hugh was exiting his window at the same time.

"Hope you two got a lot of sleep last night," Hugh smirked. "We need you in top condition to assure airworthiness of the mods—we've got to wrap this thing up!"

"Not a problem, Hugh," Clyde responded. "I am probably sharper than I have been for a number of weeks."

Hugh smiled knowingly and hurried on.

That next morning at 11:15 there was a harsh knock on the door. Clyde knew immediately that it wasn't Yumiko's knock characterized by its soft, quiet nature. When he answered the door, he was surprised and a bit concerned to see two well-dressed Japanese officials. He didn't have to invite them in before they immediately progressed through the door and into his unit.

"Oh, oh, are we in some sort of trouble?' he asked.

"No," one of them said in fairly good English. "We are here to inform you that the jury has reached its verdict. Possibly you should get your partner—a Mr. Hugh Herndon—in here so that we can explain the verdict to both of you at the same time."

Clyde said, "Sure, he's just next door. Would it be alright if we left our rooms for a moment for him to come over here?"

They indicated that it would be, so Clyde exited the room to knock on the room next door.

"Hugh, we have some visitors in my room who want your presence. Come on over to my place."

Clyde, in the meantime, was quite concerned. The two officers appeared to be very serious, but at the same time they were lenient in letting him exit his room to get Hugh. Hugh came out, and the two of them went back to Clyde's room.

The spokesman for the two addressed them. "Well, we bring you both good news and bad news. The good news is that most of the jury members believed your story and are willing to let you continue with your flight plan. There were, however, a few who felt you were imposters and very talented at making up excuses. The verdict therefore was half and half."

Now Clyde and Hugh were both very concerned. Were they going to be spared their lives or what?

"I hope you are going to tell us what this all means in simple terms," Clyde told them.

"Sure," the officer said. "We collectively decided to let you go on with your plans but will give you only one chance. This is the way of checking whether you are sincere about your ambitions or not. Your sentence will be divided into several parts. First, you will both be fined one thousand fifty dollars apiece. That must be paid within one week, or the heavier sentence will be imposed. The heavier sentence will be for each of you to spend two hundred and five days at hard labor. If your fine is paid within the week, the hard labor sentence will be waved, provided you leave Japan and never return."

"How much time do we have to prepare to leave Japan?" Clyde asked.

"You need to depart as soon as is practical. We won't specify a time, but we must be assured that you are working to depart without interruption. Oh, and by the way, if you return, your airplane will be immediately confiscated and you will both be placed under arrest—including the two hundred and five days of labor."

This sentence was imposed almost seven weeks to the day after Clyde and Hugh had first arrived in Japan.

It was quite clear to both Clyde and Hugh: a successful takeoff and en route flight the first time was absolutely imperative. This was not going to be a typical cross-country flight. There was no room for error. Once the flight was committed, they would have to go—all the way to America. They'd have only one chance for glory.

30

Back at the Ranch

Back in Boise, the Bronson family was sitting around the dinner table listening to the radio for news of the Pangborn-Herndon release from house arrest. They had been waiting for the announcement for days. Diane had been worried about their imprisonment, thinking they were confined to a jail cell and not a hotel room.

"Clyde likes his freedom," she said more than once. "Being locked up can't be easy for him."

June patted her daughter's hand. "I'm sure it isn't."

That night Diane couldn't sleep. She kept dreaming that the two were released but weren't able to make it to Misawa and then Clyde turned up at our farm in Boise wearing dirty clothes, looking like a bum. Even though she knew it was only a dream, she slept very little during the whole night.

That next morning she was assisting in the operating room—a two-year-old girl was having surgery to repair an advanced Congenital Diaphragmatic Hernia. The child, Ellen Strasser had been in and out of the hospital numerous times, and her parents—whom Diane had grown close to—were hoping the corrective surgery would make her life normal. The doctor had been straight with them. There was an excellent chance she would come through the operation fine, but there was also a slim chance that the procedure would be too much for her small fragile body.

The whole field of pediatrics was new. Children up to this time were treated as small adults until a small group of doctors recognized that there are definite anatomy differences between a developing body and one that has stabilized. Diane was supporting a Doctor Garrison whom was very active in the pediatric movement and he got her deeply interested in the field.

Diane's mind was filled with thoughts of both the child and Clyde Pangborn. The difference was that she could be of help to the little girl; there was nothing she could do for Clyde. She also knew that falling for a flier was a bad choice. Her friends had told her fliers had girlfriends in every city, and she had no reason to believe she was special to Clyde. One of her friends, Amy, who was also a nurse, had read about a girl Clyde had been involved with in Texas. Amy thought it sounded like his affair with the Texas girl hadn't ended yet.

"You better forget him," Amy said. They were drinking coffee in the hospital cafeteria, and Diane was telling Amy about her latest conversation with Clyde.

Then Amy explained, "Those aviators run around with a different woman every week. He'll only hurt you."

"He's busy with the flight and has no time for other girls. Besides, we talk as often as we can."

"Have you even gotten a letter from him since he's been in Japan?" Amy asked.

"No, but…"

It was true that even though she wrote to him every day he had yet to answer one of her letters. She told herself it was because he was so busy he didn't have the time, but when she was alone in her bedroom she feared he had forgotten her. Most of the girls that fliers were interested in followed them around like little puppy dogs. She wasn't like that. Nursing was as important to her as aviation was to Clyde. Maybe he was looking for a girl who would idolize him, not one who had a life and interests of her own.

By 6:00 a.m. she was sitting at the kitchen table eating breakfast. She didn't have to be at the hospital until 8:00, but she figured if she got there early she would spend some time with the little girl who was being operated on and maybe give her parents a break.

She was sipping a cup of coffee when she heard her mother's footsteps. A moment later June appeared in the kitchen stifling a yawn. Removing a cup from the dish drain, she poured some coffee and sat across from her daughter.

"You're up early," June said.

"I had trouble sleeping."

"Are you worried about the surgery?" June asked. "Or Clyde's flight?"

"A little bit of both, I guess," Diane said. "Mother, am I being foolish? Not about the surgery, but about Clyde. You know how men like him are—all the girls throw themselves at him. Do you think he sees me in the same way?"

"I don't know. He's the only one who can answer that question for you. Why don't you ask him the next time you see him?"

Diane paused. "I will…if there is a next time."

* * * * *

She arrived at the hospital before 7:00 and went right into little Ellen's room. Her mother was asleep in one of the chairs, and her father was watching his wife and child with the saddest expression she'd ever seen on anyone's face. Softly, she touched him on the shoulder.

He looked up at her. "Nurse Bronson, it's nice to see you, but aren't you a little early?"

"I couldn't sleep, so I decided to come in early. How is she doing?"

"She slept well all night, but I'm sorry to hear that you didn't." He smiled at her. "I guess you're worried about your boyfriend."

Diane was genuinely puzzled. "My boyfriend?"

He looked at his wife who was beginning to stir. "Yes, one of the other nurses told us that your boyfriend is getting ready to fly the Pacific. Jane thought that was very exciting. It took our minds off what's happening for a few minutes."

"Do you mean to tell me that the other nurses are gossiping about me?" Diane asked.

He was clearly embarrassed. "I hope I haven't started any trouble, because I certainly didn't mean to."

"Don't worry about it. I'll be back in a little while."

Diane had no idea that anyone at the hospital knew she was dating Clyde. Actually, they had only been out on a few dates, and she didn't consider him her boyfriend. Of course, the hospital was a hotbed of gossip, mostly about doctors and nurses that sometimes grew boring. So news that she had even gone out on one date with an aviator was exciting. But that didn't make any difference to her, because she didn't like being the center of attention. She was a private person and hated being talked about.

When she got to the nurses station, no one said anything to her and she didn't understand why. Both nurses were busy, one with medication and the other with paperwork, but they usually said a few words to her. Up until a few weeks ago, she had always been one of the most popular nurses. Could they be jealous?

"Do you have Ellen Strasser's chart?" Diane asked.

The nurse looked up at her. "I'm making a few notations. You can have it when I'm done."

She wanted things out in the open. "Which one of you has been talking to the patients about my personal life?"

"I don't understand," the nurse said.

"Mr. Strasser said something to me about 'my boyfriend.' I…"

The other nurse, who had been dividing up the patients' medications, looked up. "He came here to visit you once. I saw him with my own two eyes. Yeah, I'd say he's your boyfriend. Why aren't you in Japan for his support? I would be."

Diane thought this nurse was particularly silly. "Yes, I guess you would be, but I have patients to take care of." She turned to the other nurse. "Are you finished with Ellen Strasser's chart?"

She took the chart and went back to Ellen's room. She wasn't happy about what had just happened, or about the fact that everyone was discussing her personal life.

31

Alice Boardman

Hugh's mother, Alice Boardman, was not only a wealthy woman, she was a determined one. And in the months prior to her son and Clyde Pangborn's flight, the most important thing on her mind was making sure that flight was a success while at the same time was trying to get Hugh's wife, Mary Ellen, better acquainted within her circles. Many of her friends were wealthy and, like most everyone, they were fascinated by these new pioneers of flight. Mary Ellen, of course as interested in flight, by default, so she had some interests in common. One afternoon she was having lunch at the Russian Tea Room with some friends when an idea came to her. They were sipping iced tea and eating lobster salad, and she noticed that her good friend, Eleanor, was frowning.

"We should have gone to a speakeasy," Eleanor said. "What I wouldn't do for a glass of wine…"

Another friend Judy Garten interrupted. "I have heard that they will serve liquor here if you ask them discreetly. They bring it in flowered tea cups."

"Yes, and the next thing you know the police are here. I'd rather not risk it." She turned to Alice. "You don't look very happy, my dear. Is it Hugh?"

"Yes, it is. If the eventual flight will be such a big venture and so important to him and to me. It has to be a success, and so many things can go wrong."

"Mary Ellen seems to be coping with the situation better than you. How do you suppose she deals with it?" Eleanor asked.

"She's been brainwashed by Hugh. All of these ups and downs were explained to her as being part of the game—and she will accept anything he tells her."

"It would scare me to death to go up in the sky that way," Judy said. "Only birds are meant to fly, don't you agree?"

"No, I don't," Eleanor said. "Preston and I went last year, and it was thrilling. He liked it so much he wants to buy an airplane and hire a pilot." She glanced at Alice. "That would be a good job for Hugh."

"Hugh's his own man and doesn't want to work for anyone. But is Preston really interested in aviation?"

"Well, yes, he'd like to get involved in some way. Why do you ask?"

"I'm looking for someone, or preferably a group of people, who can oversee the help in Japan so that they will provide the best support possible. Would Preston be interested? Maybe he and some of his board of directors might be the best option. We could always use more investors, and think of what this might do for them."

Eleanor studied her friend's face. "How would my husband benefit?" she asked.

"He would benefit by the publicity, of course. Their flight so far has received worldwide attention, and when they eventually cross the Pacific and land safely in Wenatchee, which they will, there will be no stopping them. Think of Lindbergh and what his flight across the Atlantic did for him. Well, this flight will do the same for Hugh and Clyde."

Eleanor suddenly looked very interested. "I'll need to convince him. How will I do that?"

"He manufactures automobile parts. Well, now he can get in on manufacturing airplane parts. It's the wave of the future, and he'll be there from the beginning. I can't think of anything better."

32

Back in Wenatchee

Meanwhile, in Wenatchee, Clyde's brother Percy arrived at their mother Opal's house at just past 7:30 a.m. He found her sitting in an armchair in the living room listening to the radio with rapt attention. The previous night's dinner, a cheese sandwich and a glass of iced tea, were still sitting on a tray she had pushed to the side.

"Mother," Percy said. "Did you go to bed last night?"

"All that we know is that they are almost ready to be released from house arrest and will be "forced" to attempt the transpacific flight. It is rumored that they would head about two hundred miles north to a town called Misawa." Opal raised tired eyes to her son's face. "I just wish I knew something more definite, like whether or not they've gotten their airplane back and have left Tokyo."

"I know you're worried, but don't let their release and this minor flight worry you. They'll make it. You should know by now that Clyde has the ability to pull all the strings necessary to make it all happen. The real concern will be what they might do from there." He took her arm and remarked, "come on, I'll help you get into bed."

"No." She pulled her arm from his grip. "But you can put on a pot of coffee for us and bring it in here."

Percy shrugged his shoulders and went into the kitchen to prepare the coffee. While he was doing so, the phone rang, and he heard his mother speaking to someone and then suddenly raise her voice. He stopped what he was doing and went back into the living room and saw her slam the phone down into the receiver.

"That woman!"

"Who?" Percy asked.

"Mrs. Boardman, Hugh's mother. She acts like this flight was all Hugh's idea and that it will be to his credit if it's a success. It's as if Clyde has nothing to do with it and is just along for the ride. It's all because they put up the money! Rich people think they can treat poor people like they're trash. I've got a mind to call her back and tell her what I think of her."

A few minutes later Percy went into the kitchen and came back into the living room with the coffee. The two of them sat and drank as they continued to listen to the radio. There was a knock on the door. When Percy answered it, he found Sam Bennett, the editor for the *Wenatchee World,* who was a long time friend to both Clyde and himself.

"Well, speak of the devil. Do you know if they have been released yet?" Percy asked."

"There hasn't been any radio report in the last hour and a half," Sam replied. "I came over here to see if you knew something."

Suddenly, they heard Opal scream, and both rushed to her side. They found her standing in the middle of the living room jumping up and down.

"They're free, they're free. It was just announced. They're free and planning to make the trip up north to Misawa.

"Calm down, calm down Mother. That is great news, but it is only the first step. Apparently they got the airplane back as they are planning to use it for their trip to Misawa. They have a long road ahead of them to get to the place where they can consider a trip across the Pacific. Save your energy, mom, there is a lot more to come," Percy stated.

33

Following Their Release

Clyde and Hugh quickly began preparing for the flight. During this time they learned that more opportunities might have been added to the prize package. The Imperial Aeronautics Association announced additional prize money of one hundred thousand dollars, but that was limited to a Japanese team flying Japanese equipment. The Japanese newspaper prize of twenty-five thousand dollars was still intact, which might be combined with a twenty-eight thousand dollar prize being offered by the Seattle businessmen.

The Seattle businessmen's prize was first sought after by Texan barnstormer Reginald Robbins and oilman Harold Jones, who had attempted a Seattle-Tokyo flight in their Lockheed Vega on two occasions. Unfortunately, they planned to refuel in-flight using a Ford Tri-Motor tanker over Alaska and had failed on both occasions.

Another westbound attempt ended when Bob Wark was forced down just over one hundred miles from his starting point in Vancouver.

The first eastbound attempt was made just a year earlier in 1930. A Canadian pilot named Harold Fromley teamed up with the Australian navigator, Harold Gatty. They flew *City of Tacoma*, named after the city that sponsored the flight. The Emsco airplane had been built especially for the trip but was only marginally capable of the range needed for the trip. They soon returned to Japan after headwinds assured failure to reach the U.S.

Then, eventually, a young Japanese airman by the name of Seiji Yoshihara tried the crossing using an airplane with a very small engine, but engine problems put an end to that attempt.

The *City of Tacoma* Emsco airplane Fromley and Gatty brought to Japan was used in two other attempts—both by Americans. Pilot Thomas Ash failed to get the airplane off of the beach in Sabishiro, while the second attempt was made during the time Clyde and Hugh were under house arrest in Tokyo. Los Angeles salesmen Cecil Allen and Don Moyle made it off the beach but encountered mechanical difficulty and landed prematurely. After considerable hardships in trying to survive, they eventually ended up on Siberia's Kamchatka Peninsula, where they were rescued.

* * * * *

As Clyde and Hugh made their final preparations before flying to Sabishiro Beach for the takeoff, a crowd had gathered to see them off.

Then Clyde suddenly caught sight of someone in the distance. He said to Hugh, "Wait a minute. I've got some very important business to take care of." He walked in the direction of the crowd on the other side of the fence where he saw Yumiko half cheering and half crying.

Clyde knew she was sad about his leaving so he went up to her and said. "Maybe you can meet us at Sabishiro Beach," Clyde suggested. "It's quite a trip, but here is the fare you'll need to take a train there overnight." He offered her some money.

"What are my chances of going on the trip with you?" she asked.

"With all of my calculations, I suspect we will not even be able to bring along anything to eat or drink. Our weight is absolutely critical," he said.

She sobbed, and he saw the disappointment in her eyes. "I think it best we say our good-byes here," she said. "I'm too afraid to even watch your takeoff. Good luck to you both. I'll listen to the news for your progress."

He opened the fence from the inside and let her in.

After a lasting embrace, she exited the fence once again. Clyde walked toward the airplane. After about twenty paces, he turned. They both blew a kiss to each other, then Clyde returned to *Miss Veedol*.

The two aviators crawled into the cab to fly to Sabishiro Beach. It was on a Wednesday, September 30, 1931.

34

Sabishiro Beach

Using Sabishiro Beach as a transpacific departure point effectively takes two hundred miles off of the crossing distance. The beach also offered a makeshift runway with a takeoff distance of over eight thousand feet. But, to assure Japanese security, the pair and *Miss Veedol* were required to fly from Tokyo to Misawa City using a non-direct route. Approximately one hour of additional flying time was added because the airplane had to fly up the coast no less than fifty miles off shore. There was already plenty of gas in her to make this short flight.

Departing from Sabishiro Beach was not a new idea. The runway had been built years earlier for some of the other ill-fated Trans-Pacific flight attempts, including the endeavor a year earlier by Bomley and Gatty.

The takeoff field was built by the public using manual volunteer labor. Sabishiro Beach was a long stretch of fairly firm sand directed north into the prevailing wind and toward the desired departure heading. The first one thousand feet descended from a hill on the shoreline onto the beach. Over the years, the sand on the hill was leveled, packed down with a steamroller, and covered with a surface of timbers. This initial hard-surface run allowed the airplanes to accelerate to a speed where the wing was able to carry some of the weight by the time it encountered the sand. The wing lift lessened the load on the wheels, reducing their penetration into the sand. Lower sand penetration related to reduced drag during the takeoff run. The far end of the takeoff field was marked by a six-foot pile of driftwood to prevent unsuccessful airplanes from plowing into the sea.

* * * * *

Miss Veedol arrived at Sabishiro Beach at 3:00p.m. in the afternoon so the sun was beginning to settle across the Matsu-Wan bay to the west. The wind, as usual, was blowing from the North giving *Miss Veedol* an advantage in landing in the soft un-manicured sand at the make-shift runway. At the time, all of the modifications planned for the airplane were not complete, but all components needed to complete the modifications were onboard. Yosh's assistance was critical. He was able to use his heavy machining equipment needed to complete the parts required for making the modifications in Tokyo.

Upon arriving in Misawa, Clyde and Hugh were pleasantly surprised to see a rather large crowd of greeters. It was a mixed crowd. Many were official security forces and members of the Japanese Aviation Bureau to look over and maintain control of the events. Others were Americans sent by Mrs. Boardman to assist in final preparations for the flight. But most were local townspeople sincerely wishing the adventurers good luck in accomplishing their planned objectives. Of course the well-wishers included the typical contingent of young women and girls offering flowers and other gifts to the fliers. It was there that the two flyers were invited to a dinner celebration the next day sponsored by the city of Misawa. It was tradition that all flyers attempting record flights from the beach be recognized at a farewell dinner before they depart.

It was on Thursday that Hugh recognized Preston Finch and went to greet him. Preston was coordinating the U.S. working contingent sent by Mrs. Boardman. He motioned for Clyde to join them. "This is one of my mother's closest friends," Hugh said. "It's too bad we couldn't get him to back us."

Clyde's noticed the man's huge diamond pinky ring which identified him as one of Mrs. Boardman's rich friends. He wasn't sure how valuable Preston would be but he really needed the helpers he brought with him. They were trained automobile mechanics who, along with their tools could be of great help in getting *Miss Veedol* ready for the trip.

"If you plan to make another one of these flights, I might be interested in putting up some money," Preston said.

"We need to get started on this one before we can even think of another," Clyde said. "We have a lot to do, Hugh, so let's get started. You can visit Mr. Finch a little later on."

Clyde's first job was to brief the U.S. contingent who afterwards stormed the airplane to finalize the modifications.

Fuel would be loaded on *Miss Veedol* that totaled nine hundred fifteen gallons, which, along with the associated tanking and plumbing, totaled over three thousand pounds alone. The engine would run on fuel supplied from the one-hundred-eight-gallon tanks mounted in each of the wings. Those tanks would be pumped full from one hundred sixty-five gallons of fuel stowed in the belly, thirty-five gallons of fuel stowed in a chin tank built recently ahead of the belly tanks, and four hundred fifty gallons of fuel stowed in two large rectangular tanks located in the cab. In addition, about fifty gallons were put in five-gallon tins stacked in the cabin behind the large cabin tanks. The airplane was one huge flying fuel tank with wings!

Figure 17. Pulling Miss Veedol into takeoff position near Misawa

Further, oil capacity was increased to seventy-five gallons. Clyde figured flying forty hours nonstop would require the added oil capacity to help keep the engine cool.

"Hugh," Clyde said, "as copilot, you'll have the usual responsibilities, plus one extra—a very critical task."

Hugh was in a good mood. "What's that, boss man?" he asked, joking with Clyde.

"You're a comedian who knows how to pick locks," Clyde said. "Now listen, because this is important. You will be responsible for pumping fuel from these low-mounted auxiliary tanks into the main wing tanks to keep them full just as you did earlier, but we have a lot more fuel now.

The wobble pump handle is still located in the same place as before. But, because we will be adding another body tank, you will have to crawl over them from the front and into the aft compartment to operate it. While we still have the time and are on the ground, I'd like you to go through the operation just to be sure that it is possible. Just pretend that the new full tank is installed here in this area."

Clyde outlined with his hands, the volume that will be taken up by the new tank.

Hugh stood up in the front seat and laid his upper body over the existing large tank.

"I look pretty good, don't I?" Hugh asked. "Let's take a picture and send it to the newspapers."

"Do you take anything seriously?" Clyde asked.

"Okay, I'm being serious now. Maybe I can pull myself over somehow. Oh, I can reach the pump handle from here. Let's see if I can use it to pull myself over. That works, but now I have to swing myself down into the aft cab. I can do it now, but it might be more difficult when the back is full of five-gallon gas tins. It will be hard to see the fuel gauges way up there in the root."

"You'll have to find a way to constantly watch those gages for the upper tanks to be sure they are full, obviously," Clyde replied.

"Okay, Clyde, I'll figure something out."

Just as a trial, Hugh raised his head from his current position to view the fuel gauges. "I can't see the gauges from here," he said. "Let me crawl in the back and see if I can see them"

Hugh moved over the tanks and into the aft compartment to get a better look. "There they are, but you have to work at it to see them clearly," he said.

"Well, keep an eye on them and don't forget, or we will be dead in the water. Oops, what a morbid pun," Clyde said.

Later, as the team readied the airplane, Clyde and Hugh peeked in the side window. "Oh, they loaded the small tins," Clyde told Hugh. "The individual five-gallon tins will have to be handled separately. During the initial part of the trip, they are located aft, which will help us get off the beach with this extremely heavy load—but they are a nuisance as they are in the way for you to operate the wobble pump."

Just about then, a group of three mechanics came with the pieces to the added floor-mounted fuel tank and began fitting them carefully though the aft zippered window. They knew that they would fit as they just removed them to conduct a fit-check outside. Clyde and Hugh backed away so as not to interfere with progress.

Clyde explained, "You need to get rid of those five-gallon tins first. To do that, you will have to make volume available in the large tanks to accommodate this fuel by pumping some of the fuel up into the wing using the wobble pump."

Clyde animated the motions that would be necessary to Hugh so that he could better understand.

He added, "Then you can transfer the fuel from the tins into the two installed floor tanks using this siphon which we need to store someplace conveniently. Where can we put this so that it is out of the way but somewhere where we'll both know where it is?"

Clyde stuck his head inside to look for a storage spot.

"Here, let's lash it down to the top of the tank right here were you can reach it from the front or the back," he said

"Eventually, you'll have to pump all of the fuel up above using the wobble pump."

Hugh nodded.

"A big problem will be getting rid of the empty tins," Clyde said. "You can throw them out of the zippered door—they'll fit, but just barely. I'd show you right now, but those windows are in use by the mechanics. We have got to be careful, though, as that door is located directly ahead of our tail surfaces. –see."

They moved to the back of the airplane and Clyde animated the can leaving the zippered window and striking the horizontal tail.

"Before you release them, give me a signal, and I'll put the airplane into a hard sideslip at low speed to help the tin miss the tail—is that clear?"

Hugh replied, "I don't see any problem. But because we cannot hear each other, you'll have to be aware ahead of time so you can be watching for my signal."

"Just let me know before you head on back to transfer fuel from the small tins, so I can watch out for you. We will also have to be extremely careful about controlling the location of the center of gravity. I'll help advise you of where you can place your own body mass to begin with until we get settled down in a more unconstrained cruise mode.

Just about then, it started to rain. The spectator crowd began to thin and the work crew conveniently found refuge under the wing.

"This is an on-going threat this time of year. We will just have to find a way to keep working during these weather changes," one of the workers said.

"Fuel management is probably one of the most demanding chores en route," Clyde told Hugh. "Not only do we need to assure that the upper wing tanks are always full, we need to be sure that fuel is transferred from the proper tanks to keep the center of gravity located within the limits of the airplane aerodynamic capabilities. You are in charge."

"I'll try," Hugh said.

"You have to do better than that, Hugh! You have to do the job perfectly," Clyde said. "I will have my hands full with flying, navigation, and engine monitoring, except during rest periods when I'll have to ask for your assistance."

"I'll do everything I can," Hugh said. "This flight is as important to me as it is to you."

Clyde patted him on the back. "I hope so, Hugh. It'll be a matter of life and death!"

Hugh laughed. "If we aren't successful, I'll never hear the end of it from my mother. Just that alone is motivation for me."

By Friday, October 2, the final adjustments were being made. The propeller had a manually adjustable pitch that could be set anywhere from flat for optimum takeoff performance to full open for optimum cruise performance. That adjustment had to be done on the ground with no variation possible once the engine was running, which meant that Clyde had a major decision to make. He needed the best cruise performance to travel the distance to America, but he would have a challenging takeoff to get this heavy load off of the beach in Japan. He compromised toward the flat pitch for takeoff, realizing that he would pay a cruise penalty of nearly five percent in range.

* * * * *

The Japanese Aviation Bureau spent the better part of Friday, carefully going over the airplane and its modifications. Their responsibility was to assure that the airplane was prepared to safely make an attempt to cross the Pacific. It was heavily overloaded, but the members of the division had no knowledge beyond what Clyde had used to prepare the airplane for flight. It wasn't known if the airplane structure or flying capabilities could handle this excessive weight, so substantial study and calculations were required. Their studies completely overwhelmed them to the point where subsystems such as that installed to eject the landing gear were easily overlooked. By the end of the day, they approved the airplane and signed it off for its record attempt.

Clyde shook hands with the supervisors in charge of the inspection and quickly gathered his people together in a private location off to one side. "I am relieved to reach this approval stage and want to thank the entire team for their dedicated effort. I'd like to get this flight underway within the next several days—the weather will only get worse as winter approaches. It is obvious that you guys did an excellent job at disguising the gear release mechanism so that the Japanese had no clue that such a system existed."

The next day, Saturday, October 3, the team worked feverously to get prepared for the flight. Japanese bystanders along with a small number of official Japanese guards watched over the airplane and the flight proceedings. Some spent a great deal of time near the airplane, where they couldn't keep from looking over the details of the airframe. Suddenly, it was apparent that one guard who had some aircraft design expertise spotted the unusual mechanism leading to the landing gear support structure. He asked some of the U.S. citizens about the reason for the mechanism and was given a polite shoulder shrug in every case.

He said, "Who is in charge of this flight?"

Workers in the area had no choice but to answer, "Clyde Pangborn. He's over there."

The guard immediately approached Clyde and exclaimed, "Are you Clyde Pangborn?" in a broken English.

Clyde replied, "Yes, sir, what can I do for you?"

"I want to understand more about the cables I see coming out of the bottom of the airplane leading to the landing gear," he said.

"Oh, those things," Clyde said. "They are just something they put on in the factory to monitor the temperature of the brakes during heavy braking."

"I don't believe that!" he shouted. "Those are not electrical wires. They're some sort of control cables! I will not allow you to take off until we review this further next week!"

"That will simply delay us for no reason," Clyde responded. "Why are those so important to you?"

"We cannot allow any unapproved system on the airplane, and I am sure that this is a system that we have not inspected," the guard said.

Clyde's fear was that an in-depth review could lead to a significant change in their plans that could lead to catastrophic failure in reaching the U.S.

To defuse the conversation, Clyde told the guard, "We will try to set something up on Monday, okay?"

The guard acknowledged him and went on his way.

As luck would have it, it was early in the weekend, and the authorities were not on duty. The low-level guard on duty did not have the authority to call the board together during that time, nor was he able to make a decision to delay the flight independently. Clyde felt immediate pressure to take off before the end of the weekend to avoid any further questioning.

"Let's get our stuff together, Hugh, and get ready to shove off." Clyde said.

"No problem, my material is onboard except for the final navigation charts, which I worked up late last night. I'll go get them," Hugh responded.

35

More Problems

Moments later, Hugh could be heard shouting, "They're gone! They're gone!"

"What's gone?" Clyde responded.

"All of my navigation charts showing the routes and en route way-points—you know how critical they are," he said.

"Look again. Maybe you put them someplace else."

"No way, I kept close track of them because of their importance," Hugh said.

Just then, one of the maintenance crew stepped forward and suggested that he'd seen a suspicious individual working in that area near where the charts were kept that morning. There were several Japanese helping out, but this particular one was not among the ones officially approved.

"I cannot believe that anyone would have any interest whatsoever in our charts," Clyde said. "They are useless to anyone but us."

"We have a radical political group known as the Black Dragon Society that is violently opposed to any non-Japanese group attempting this record—especially with non-Japanese equipment," said one of the local helpers. "It may be an attempt to scuttle your flight."

"Well, he—or they—knew where the vital links were," Clyde said. "They obviously know that in order to set a record time or distance, a great circle route must be adhered to religiously. To fly from Japan to the U.S., the crew cannot simply fly straight East—that is the long way around. A direct compass route is all but useless. A great circle route must be laid out and waypoints established along the way."

Clyde stretched out his arms and formed a big circle with is finger tips. "Remember, the world is round. The shortest distance to the U.S. is a line passing way up north of here into the Bering Sea," as he pointed northward in a direction obviously not in the direction across the Pacific.

"We'll have to travel north from here, across the Aleutian Chain, and then southwest along the coast of Alaska and Canada. Careful navigation from waypoint to waypoint is a major task. The charts that were taken have all of the intermediate waypoints identified to make the trip—that information is vital!

"Okay, we have a crisis. Hugh, organize everyone here to search for the old charts and start to reconstruct a new set for backup in case we fail to locate them. We will have to delay our departure until we have something that we can rely on—but we have to get out of here this weekend. I have one more chore to do in the meantime. I'll work on that while you try to gather up some charts."

* * * * *

On Saturday Hugh's team was busy working up new charts, and *Miss Veedol* was set for takeoff. A skeleton crew of Japanese security and aeronautical authorities, including the one troublesome guard, meandered around the area as they were assigned to cover the weekend.

Clyde wanted to take a closer look at the so-called runway extending over the beach. He noticed earlier that most of it would support the airplane properly, but there were some soft spots that might cause them a problem. He gathered up a handful of short sticks, tore up an old shirt into strips, and tied a short cloth flag on the end of each of the sticks. He also made a wooden block measuring three square inches of surface, which he tied to the bottom of one foot. With the small flags and this wooden block under his foot, he proceeded to walk the length of the runway toward the stack of logs off in the distance.

He had calculated that his weight concentrated on the three square inches was about equivalent to the eighty pounds per square inch tire pressure supporting *Miss Veedol*. As he walked, he was able to judge areas on the beach that were relatively hard and areas that were relatively soft. He stuck one of the small flags in the sand near each of the apparent soft spots. After walking the full length of the runway three times, he had a fairly good idea of the areas he must avoid during takeoff.

On his forth trip down the field, he asked Tom, another one of the Americans sent to Japan by Mrs. Boardman, to join him. Clyde had Tom drag a large snag tied to a rope behind him as he followed Clyde down the runway along a route that avoided the small flags. Clyde wanted to make a path that would avoid the soft spots but not be impossible to follow during the takeoff run.

Once the two reached the pile of logs on the far end of the runway, they found it to be over six feet high. Each grabbed the logs one at a time and rearranged them so that the height was reduced in half to three feet.

Clyde told Tom, "now I hope that wasn't necessary but the reduced height provides just a little bit of margin—for a very marginal takeoff. If the three foot improvement we just made is needed, the airplane would be hardly flying.

Then, on return, Tom dragged the snag again, marking the extreme on the other side of the runway that avoided the soft spots.

Once they reached the airplane, there still remained a fairly large group of local well-wishers. Clyde asked one of them, who he earlier found served as a good interpreter, to check for volunteers who might want to help out. He was surprised to find over one hundred people ready to step out of the crowd to assist in any way possible. Clyde was impressed by the support he received from the local folks.

Clyde asked his interpreter to organize the large group so that they could stomp on the sand between the corduroy ramp and the pile of logs following the path left by the snag they had dragged over the desired takeoff route. For the next four hours, dozens of volunteers stomped and jumped all over the beach to pack down the sand.

While the volunteers worked on the runway, Clyde looked over the heavy loaded airplane and was concerned that the tires were bulging from the excessive weight. Even with the recommended inflation pressure, it was obvious that they were well beyond their design load. A higher tire pressure would improve the tire overload but exert an even higher loading on the delicate sand surface. After much consideration, Clyde believed they would be good for at least one takeoff at the existing lower tire pressure. After that, he planned to jettison the gear so that the tires only had to survive the single abusive run.

By Sunday morning, October fourth, acceptable charts had been produced, the runway was prepared, and the airplane was ready to be pulled to the top of the hill marking the start of the runway.

Clyde pulled his U.S. contingent aside to give them a status on their effort to get *Miss Veedol* into the air. "This airplane is one heavy dude," Clyde said. "We will be taking off with the highest gross weight ever attempted in the Bellanca—hope she can do it! To take all precautions, we will have to offload everything we can just to keep the weight down. Let's throw out all survival equipment, extra clothing, seat cushions, and even our boots."

Fritz, an American foreign correspondent girl who was there to help out, was, among other things, in charge of in-flight food. She had indicated that she planned a fairly substantial chicken dinner for the two to share on the way.

Clyde explained, "Fritz, about that chicken dinner—make it just a few pieces of chicken and a little tea to wash it down. That is all the weight we can afford."

Even so, with nine hundred fifteen gallons of fuel and seventy-five gallons of oil onboard, the Bellanca was taking off with a gross weight of over nine thousand pounds—over one and one-half tons beyond the maximum structural takeoff gross weight specified by Giuseppe Bellanca.

Just as Hugh and Clyde were prepared to climb into the windows of the awaiting *Miss Veedol*, a small Japanese boy broke free of the crowd barriers and rushed to them carrying something in his arms. The two hesitated for a moment and found the boy carrying five apples that he picked from his fathers orchard. This had a special meaning to Clyde as his hometown of Wenatchee, Washington was also famous for being a major supplier of apples. Apparently the boy's father knew this and offered the gift as an expression of friendship.

36

Diane's Worried

After accepting his gift of apples, Clyde was ready to depart back to his homeland and his warm relationship with Diane. He wondered what she was doing while he was about ready to depart. *If all goes well, and I assume it will, I'll see her in a few days. Of course it is a long way from Boise to Wenatchee, but maybe she will hear of our departure and be on her way to Wenatchee before we get there...*

Because there was a seventeen-hour time difference between Japan and the northwest, Diane would be fast asleep in the middle of the night. Ten hours earlier she was driving home from work with her good friend Jeanne. She turned the radio on, and soon they were listening to "Goodnight, Sweetheart," one of Diane's favorite songs.

"Don't you love this song?" Diane asked. "It's so romantic."

Jeanne laughed. "I guess you've got romance on your mind. Me? I've got a paper to write on anatomy in two days, and I haven't put a word on paper. You're so lucky you graduated already."

"I'm assisting Dr. Garrison in his hernia surgery tomorrow. Pretty scary."

"Ellen Strasser?" Jeanne asked.

"Yes, poor little girl. The doctor has already told us it's going to be rough. He gave her a very good chance of recovery but not one hundred percent. The mother broke down and sobbed." Diane said, " I love nursing, but..."

"I know. It makes you question everything," Jeanne said. "Why would God give this little girl life only to play games with it."

"She has every chance of surviving, and I know that Dr. Garrison will do everything he can to make the procedure a success," Diane replied.

"But that's not the only thing you have on your mind, is it? Are you going to tell me about this guy or keep everything a secret even from your best friend?" Jeanne teased her.

Diane laughed. "There's nothing like a good mystery."

"Mysteries stink," Jeanne said and poked her playfully. "I'm your best friend, and I have the right to know what's going on in your life."

She pushed her softly with her right hand.

"You can read about Clyde in the newspapers or, better still, wait until he lands in Washington. Then you can find out everything you want to know about him," Diane replied.

"But not about you and him. Is it serious?"

"I don't think so. We've been on a few dates, and I enjoy his company even though he is kind of quiet and shy. His main interest is aviation, and he doesn't care about much else. And since I'm mostly interested in nursing, I think we're kind of boring together. He needs someone more outgoing who can bring him out of his shell." Diane admitted.

"So, are you saying it's over between the two of you?" Jeanne asked.

"No, I'm saying we may not be right for each other."

"Are you in love with him?" Jeanne asked.

"I don't know. I've been asking myself the same question."

Before long, Diane was scrubbing up for surgery. The surgeon, Dr. Garrison, who had performed more operations than any other surgeon in Idaho, was in his fifties. He treated Diane in a fatherly manner like he did all young nurses. She wanted this to be a learning experience for herself, but her head was so filled with Clyde that she was afraid she would loose the opportunity.

She never wanted to be one of those girls who thought about nothing other than men—how to meet one, how to get one to fall in love with you and get married. Like other women Diane wanted to fall in love and marry, but she didn't want to become obsessed with the idea. Her parents didn't push her, either, even though at twenty-one many of her girlfriends were married and having babies. Diane's parents had encouraged her to pursue nursing and believed in everything she wanted to do. They supported her relationship with Clyde, too, although they were concerned that she would be hurt.

When the doctors and nurses and anesthesiologist had finished scrubbing up, they entered the operating theatre. As the full team moved about the room, Ellen Strasser laid on the table, looking so tiny and helpless that the sight of her brought tears to Diane's eyes. The little girl's blue eyes were wide open, and she looked frightened and confused. Diane went to her side and brushed her blonde bangs away from her forehead.

"In a little while you'll go to sleep and dream of lollipops and candy," Diane said. "When you wake up, you will be all well again and can plan what you want to do next year in school."

"Will you stay with me?"

Diane held back the tears. "And I'll be here when you wake up too."

Though it took four grueling hours, the operation was a success. By four o'clock in the afternoon, Ellen was back in the ICU and her parents were sitting at her bedside holding her hands. Diane gently touched Mrs. Strasser on the shoulder, and the girl's mother turned around and looked at Diane with such gratitude in her eyes that Diane nearly wept.

"Has the doctor spoken to you?" she asked.

"He was here a little while ago and told us everything seems to be going fine."

"She did beautifully during surgery and should be fine. Her recovery should not be long, and when it's over, she'll be a perfectly healthy normal child."

Diane looked at the child for a few more minutes and then walked out of the room. This was what life was all about—the connection between husband and wife, parent and child. It was what she had with her mother, father, and brother and what she knew she would never have with Clyde. His connection was to the sky, and no one would ever be able to compete with that.

37

The Mothers' Dilemma

Meanwhile, Hugh was the center of Alice Boardman's mind. She and Hugh's wife Mary Ellen arrived at the large, imposing house of Preston and Eleanor Finch for dinner that evening still not knowing whether Hugh had taken off. The invitation had been a surprise, and Alice knew that Eleanor had sent it to get their minds off what was happening in Japan.

"How are you doing, Alice?" Eleanor asked, kissing her cheek. "It's good to see you. Oh, and Mary Ellen, I haven't seen you for some time—how are you holding up?"

Mary Ellen replied, "fairly well, all of this excitement is new to me. Hugh left on the trip just five days after we were married, you know."

Judy and Paul Garten walked into the room. Paul extended his hand and Alice shook it. Then she and Judy hugged briefly.

"We're glad to see you," Judy said.

"I'm glad we're having dinner together," Eleanor said. "Alice, I'm sure you and Mary Ellen will be sitting in front of the radio waiting to hear news about Hugh."

"That reminds me; turn the radio on, Eleanor. I want to make sure I don't miss anything."

"Do you know if they've taken off yet?" Paul asked.

Alice sighed. "If one more person asks me that question, I'm going to scream. You'd think that as Hugh's mother someone would tell me something, but no one has. What about your husband, Eleanor? Has he called you?"

"No. Do you want me to call his hotel room and see if he's there and can tell us something?"

"Do you need to ask?"

Everyone followed Eleanor into her husband's study and watched while she sat down at his desk. It took several minutes before the overseas operator managed to connect them to the hotel. Luckily the manager spoke English, and soon the phone began to ring in Preston's hotel room. Eleanor handed the phone to Alice, who yelled into the receiver.

"What's going on, Pres?" she asked.

"There's no need to yell; I can hear you just fine," Preston said.

"What do you know?" Alice said. "You're a million miles away. So what are you waiting for? Have they taken off yet? Tell me what's going on."

"Neither your son nor Mr. Pangborn would say two words to me. Hugh just told me to get out of the way, so I did. I came back to the hotel and am planning to get out of this damn country as soon as I can."

"No, you aren't," Alice said. "Go back to Sabishiro Beach and tell me everything that happens. Take notes if you have to."

"What the hell do you think I am, your goddamn secretary? *You* get over here and take notes."

"Won't you even go back to the beach and make sure the takeoff goes smoothly?" Alice said demurely. "What if it was your son, Preston?"

"I'll go, but only because you're a friend. When did Hugh become so rude, Alice?"

"He has a lot on his mind. We'll make it up to you, I promise."

There was a large, elaborate baby grand piano in the Finch's living room that Eleanor treated like a child. Whenever there were guests in the house, she showed it off to them, even if they had seen it dozens of times before. Then she began to pour the champagne while conversing with Alice about Hugh. Since she and Preston didn't have any children, she had always treated Hugh as a son and was as worried about him as Alice.

"It's great to share fine food and good wine with friends," Eleanor said. She raised her glass. "Cheers."

Everyone responded with the clinking of glasses, and more conversations began, mostly about Clyde's and Hugh's flight and whether or not it would be a success. Alice was surprised by how many people still thought aviation was a waste of time.

The early evening sun was bright, throwing distinct shadows and enhancing the colors in the formal dining room. Eleanor had an eye for decorating, and Alice often sought her advice if she wanted to redecorate. The dining room table elegantly displayed expensive crystal glasses, powder blue napkins folded in the perfect manner, and elegant name-place cards. *All this,* Alice thought, *is in honor of my son.*

"This meal is extraordinary," Alice said as they began the first course, lobster bisque.

Eleanor nodded. Since the phone call to Preston, Alice had noticed that Ellie seemed preoccupied and wondered why.

"Well, I can't take credit for it," Eleanor said. "I had the whole thing catered. You really don't think my culinary skills are up to these standards, do you?

They were halfway through the meal when Paul Garten raised his glass and toasted Hugh.

"To a safe journey," Paul said.

Almost as an afterthought, Alice said, "Let's not forget his friend, Clyde Pangborn. They're in this thing together, and the success depends as much on Clyde as it does Hugh."

They raised their glasses again and made another toast, this time to both men.

38

News Reaches Wenatchee

There was a lot going on in Masawa, but the word was slow in getting around—especially to the little town of Wenatchee, Washington. Opal Pangborn's house was in a quiet neighborhood and set back a little from the road. It was small, only five rooms, but it was the perfect size for her. Since the early days, having traveled across the country in a covered wagon as a baby, she felt like she was living in luxury. She had a stove and an ice box, and with the ice man coming every day she only had to shop for food every other day. She loved to go on little errands because she would meet friends and talk about this or that, usually her sons. She lived for them. During the last two days Opal hadn't left the house, but her friends weren't concerned. They knew she was waiting to hear whether or not her son Clyde had finally taken off from Japan on his attempt to cross the Pacific, non-stop. Every couple of hours someone would call, and the ensuing conversation was always the same.

"Have you heard anything?" the friend would ask.

"Not yet," Opal would say and then hang up the phone.

And so it went.

One of Opal's friends had once said she could win a prize for organization. On the spur of the moment, she decided to invite about twenty-five members of the press for lunch while she waited to hear if Clyde and Hugh had taken off yet. She had kept a notebook with the names of all the reporters in Wenatchee and the surrounding areas who had reported on Clyde's career. She called each one of them herself and invited them to lunch. Percy was amazed by the fact that she'd gotten no sleep and still had so much energy.

"It's all adrenaline," his mother told him.

The luncheon was set for one afternoon. Opal listened to the radio intently, still waiting for news while she vacuumed the rugs and dusted the furniture. She sent Percy out to pick up the ingredients for lunch: BLTs and homemade split pea soup.

While she was making the soup, the news came that Clyde and Hugh were within minutes of taking off. Opal, never a religious woman, made the sign of the cross and said a silent prayer.

"Mother, I think you should rest for a few minutes," Percy said. "This is all too much for you."

"Stop babying me. I'm fine. I've got twenty-five hungry reporters to feed who will be here in an hour. I have no time to sit and do nothing."

"Sixteen reporters, remember? Nine of them couldn't come," Percy said.

"I know. I just want to make extra because they'll probably be hungry." She pointed to one of the kitchen cabinets. "Take the good white dishes and set the table in the dining room. You'll need the extension. It's in the hall closet."

Like a dutiful son, Percy retrieved the extension and put the table together. By the time the reporters arrived, the table was set with all Opal's best dishes, and she was wearing her Sunday dress. In fact she thought that she looked like she was going to church.

There was only one female reporter among the group, and Opal had insisted she come. Even though the woman wasn't a news reporter, Opal thought that as a mother she would understand the story better than the male reporters.

Then the crowd started to arrive. The yard looked like a parking lot outside of a Sears Roebuck Store.

When her neighbor Mrs. McCrady knocked on the door just as they were about to sit down, Opal got annoyed. She parted the living room curtains and saw the old woman, who must have been well into her eighties, waving and pointed at all the cars.

"What's going on?" Mrs. McCrady asked after Opal answered the door.

"We're having a discussion about my son's flight," Opal said. "You know he's about to make history."

Mrs. McCrady pointed to Percy. "He's right over there. Honestly, Opal, you are very strange at times."

"I'm talking about my other, son, Clyde. Don't you read the newspaper?"

"What other son? You never told me about him."

Opal shook her head. "You've met him. Would you like to stay for lunch?"

Mrs. McCrady looked around the room. "OK, as long as I can sit next to you. Those men," she said, indicating the reporters, "look dangerous, don't you think? Are they from the FBI?"

They sat down at the table and everyone dug into their soup. The radio was playing in the background, and everyone was waiting to hear the announcement that *Miss Veedol* had taken off.

Glenn Yardley said, "How confident are you that this flight will be a success, Mrs. Pangborn?"

Opal sighed and passed the rolls to Percy, who was sitting next to her. "I'm very confident that it will be a success. Right now the most frustrating part is wondering what's happening. Have any of you heard anything?"

"I'm afraid not," Yardley said. "If we had, we'd have told you."

They continued to eat, and the ensuing conversation was about the flight: the dangers, and what the aftereffects might be, including how Clyde's life might change.

"He isn't looking for fame," Opal insisted. "The most important thing to him is to bring aviation to the forefront of people's lives and show them how they can benefit from it."

Opal looked around the table and saw that the reporters were writing in their notepads. It was a comforting thought knowing that Clyde's wishes would be on the front page of the newspaper tomorrow morning. It was what he wanted. He had experienced enough turbulence of late, and after the flight he would need a period of complete and total peace. She intended to make sure he found that peace.

She was about to bring out the coffee and pie when the phone rang. Having no idea who it was, she went to answer it. The radio was still on, and she was trying to listen to it and the caller at the same time. A stranger's voice responded when she answered.

"Whom am I speaking to?" Opal asked.

"This is Diane Bronson, Clyde's friend. Have you heard whether or not he's taken off? We've been waiting to hear, but we figured you would know before we do."

Opal smiled. Diane sounded like a lovely girl, and Clyde had pretty much told her the same thing.

"We're waiting to hear too, Diane. I guess news travels slowly from Japan to the United States. But don't you worry. Everything is going to be fine."

"I know you're right," Diane said. "It's just that…" her voice trailed off.

Opal wondered if she was going to say she loved Clyde and would have been delighted if she had. Like any other mother she wanted him to settle down and have a family, and she knew he wanted to also. But he lived the life of a nomad, and she didn't know if he would ever be a family man.

"He's very fond of you, you know," Opal said. "He doesn't let just anyone beat him at chess. He told me you're quite a chess player."

Diane laughed. "I beat him once, that's all."

"Diane, I have to go, I have lunch guests. We'll keep in touch. I'm sure there'll be news soon."

* * * * *

During Clyde's last visit with Diane they discovered they both liked to play chess, which was a surprise to Diane. After they played a game, they had walked around the farm grounds and Clyde told her that one of his ambitions was to own and run a farm.

An odd thought came into her mind. What if they lived on the farm together and ran it together? Of course, they couldn't do so unless they were married, and Clyde had never given her any indication that he was even remotely thinking of marrying her or anyone else. The only thing he ever talked about was his flight around the world.

After her phone conversation with Opal, Diane opened the book she was reading and read half a chapter about caring for children with rheumatic hearts. She and Clyde were alike in the sense that they were both obsessed with their work, but that didn't leave much room for anything else in their lives.

A few months from now, when the flight was behind him, what place would she have in Clyde Pangborn's life? Diane knew her mother didn't think they were right for each other. June liked Clyde but didn't think their relationship would go anywhere. After this flight Diane felt certain he would seek to break some other record. Could she ever hope to have a relationship with someone with such ambitions?

39

Back in Japan

In Japan, the excitement was garnering. It was Sunday, October 4, 1931. The onlookers gathered by the hundreds in anticipation of the takeoff. The days of preparation had been difficult for Clyde and Hugh, especially their imprisonment, but now that the moment had come they were both excited. They both thought of the flight, but their minds also focused on the people they cared about—Clyde's thoughts were with his mother, brother, Diane, and Yumiko, wondering if he'd ever see any of them again. Hugh wondered if Mary Ellen missed him as much as he missed her. He was also certain that his mother was giving everyone around her a hard time.

Figure 18. Locals biding farewell to the flying team

Clyde calculated and recalculated the takeoff and cruise performance a number of times. Their flight was critical throughout so that if any adverse winds were encountered, success could still be marginally achieved. Since he was technically oriented, he was able to deduct the advantages and disadvantages of almost all variables. He knew that the speed needed to take off from the beach would have to be at least ninety miles per hour. He also knew that the flight after takeoff would be marginal until weight was burned off or drag could be reduced by dropping the gear.

Time was rapidly passing and the two knew that they must be on their way. They did need daylight to land at the other end of the forty or so hour trip, so they calculated a late day departure from Japan was beneficial. But they also knew that they could not delay into the work week starting the next day. So the time is now.

Everything had to be done to maximize the chances of a successful takeoff. The engine had to be revved to full power before brake release. To do this, a rope was tied to the tail wheel and to a steel spike driven into the ramp behind the airplane. Takeoff release would be made by cutting the rope at Clyde's command.

After considering all of the alternatives, he turned to Hugh.

"Let's hop on in, Hugh. It's time to go."

For a few seconds they stared at each other. "You're sure?" Hugh asked. "We are fifty percent over weight. Will the structure hold together? Is the engine operating at peak performance—and even if it is, can it lift this heavy weight off of the beach sands? Will the tires hold up the load? Or might they sink into the sand—or blow up for that matter? And if all that goes well, how sure are we that the modifications we made will get us across the pond? We'll certainly be working the *Pangborn Factor* overtime, so I hope that the powers to be are looking over us!"

"I am. It's time," Clyde nodded in reassurance.

The two quickly said their good-byes to all of their friends who directly aided in getting the airplane ready; the

Figure 19. Reading Miss Veedol for takeoff on planked runway at Sabishiro Beach near Misawa

American contingent, the Japanese volunteers and the Japanese officials. Clyde stood on a high pile of sand near the end of the runway and humbly thanked the entire crowd for being there and offering their support. He and Hugh then crawled through the open cab windows and prepared to depart. The airplane was already aligned with the runway. One of the ground crew climbed onto the forward strut and, by force of habit, hollered, "Breaks!"

Clyde responded, "Check the tie-down rope!"

A ground crew member quickly checked the rope and signaled a thumbs-up to Clyde and the crew member on the side of the airplane.

Just then, Clyde spotted a man some five hundred feet down the corduroy ramp dragging driftwood into the takeoff path. By this time, a fairly large amount of material had been stacked, making it impossible to depart. Clyde took a closer look and realized the man was the "low-level" guard who insisted on delaying the flight until the aviation bureau could have a review of the strange sub-system he previously spotted on the airplane.

Clyde yelled out the window, "What is that guy doing?"

Clyde was disgusted. One thing after another had prevented them from taking off, and now there was something else. Now how long would they have to wait? He knew Hugh's patience was running out too.

Just then, a group of eleven local Japanese men took off running toward the guard. Four grabbed the guard and pulled him off the side of the runway and held him down while the others quickly began to clear the ramp. In five minutes, the path was cleared, and one of the men motioned to begin the takeoff. Clyde and Hugh grinned at each other, both relieved.

The ground crew member on the side of the airplane began to spin up the internal inertia flywheel to start the WASP engine. Soon, they pulled the release and the prop began to spin. One piston fired, a puff of smoke emerged, and the engine noisily came to life.

Clyde told Hugh, "The oil pressure is up, the mags are working, she seems to take throttle alright." He revved the engine up several times. "I hope you are all buckled up, because we are ready to leave this place."

Clyde opened the throttle to the full open position. Sand flew behind the airplane while the onlookers held their breath in excitement.

Clyde motioned to cut the rope and yelled over the roar of the engine, "Here we go!"

40

The Takeoff

Clyde headed *Miss Veedol* directly down the wooden planks toward the beach. Thump, thump, thump went the plane across the corduroy ramp. It wasn't the smoothest ride, but it was effective as the speed quickly accelerated to fifty miles per hour before reaching the sand. When the airplane leaped onto the sand, their heads snapped forward as the rapid acceleration decreased when the wheels began to mire into the softer sand.

Clyde followed the path stomped in the sand and started to gently rock the airplane from side to side using the ailerons. By swaying the airplane this way he could unstick one side at the expense of putting more weight on the other side, but the net effect helped lighten the airplane on the sand.

"Sixty miles per hour!" Hugh shouted.

"Hang on, we are starting to plane to the top of the sand," Clyde responded.

"Seventy miles per hour—those logs at the end of the runway are coming up fast!" Hugh shouted. "Eighty miles per hour…eighty five…ninety…lift off Clyde, lift off! I'll pull the fuel jettison lever!"

"No, Hugh, leave that damn lever alone! The airplane isn't ready to fly yet! We are going to pile into that stack of logs or fly over them. I don't intend on staying another day in Japan."

"One hundred miles per hour!"

Just then, Clyde was able to pull back on the yoke enough to barely skim over the three-foot pile of logs and was airborne. Out of the corner of his eye, he spotted a small figure with waving arms far out on the beach. It was Yumiko waving her last farewell to the flying team. Someday, Clyde hoped he'd see her again.

As they passed the log obstacle, the airplane again settled down to a lower height just over the water.

Clyde explained, "Man, we really had the weight calculated right down to the pound! The airplane was too heavy to fly in free air, so it is settling down into ground effect. As long as we stay within a one-half wingspan distance above the water, we'll benefit from reduced induced drag, allowing us to stay airborne. We'll have to burn off some fuel to reduce our weight before we can begin our climb in free air above the surface of the water."

"Why don't we jettison our landing gear? Won't that help?" Hugh asked.

"It sure would, Hugh, but we might need that gear yet. I'd like to keep it with us until we are sure that our Pacific crossing is a go."

Clyde was in control. His years of stunt flying taught him the techniques of flying close to stall and in adverse speed stability regimes. He knew that the worst thing he could do was to make turns or attempt to climb under these conditions. His biggest concern was the dips and the valleys between the waves on the ocean surface. Luckily, this was a calm day and the water was fairly stable.

"Now, Hugh," Clyde shouted over the sound of the engine. "This is what you have to do. We need to start getting fuel transferred out of those tins back there into the main tanks and start transferring fuel up into the main wing tanks. We need to do a little center-of-gravity control and start getting our fuel into the upper tanks. At this high power we need to maintain, we are probably burning a gallon every two minutes."

"I'll jump into the back and go to work," Hugh said.

"Hang on, Hugh, not yet. Our center of gravity is already far aft. We can't get it too far back or I won't be able to control the instability that might cause. Maybe you can lie over the body tanks and work the wobble pump long enough to transfer some of the fuel out of the body tanks to make space for fuel from the tins. Once you are confident that there is adequate empty volume in them, hopefully you can grab one of the tins and transfer the fuel from up here first. If you can get a few of the tins out of the back emptied forward, then maybe that will allow you to move your weight back there. Then when you are able to get into the back, you will have to pump the wobble pump like hell to get the wing tanks refilled. We'll have to keep the empty tins onboard for a while until we burn off more fuel and gain more performance margin."

"Okay, Clyde, I'll give it a try."

Hugh laid over the body tanks, grabbed the wobble pump handle, and began to pump. The small pump required constant pumping for at least ten minutes to make any significant fuel increase in the upper tanks. Once the fuel transfer was done, however, he was able to reach into the back with much effort and pull the forty-pound tin onto the tank top next to him. The siphon tube arrangement was also nearby, which he was able to get unlashed from the top of the tank. With some inconvenience, fuel was being siphoned out of the tin into the main body tank.

Hugh was able to transfer four tins in this manner and throw the empties into the back. This took the better part of an hour, which meant another thirty to forty pounds more fuel was also being burned off.

"Hugh, move into the back slowly, but try to keep your weight as far forward as possible!" Clyde yelled.

Hugh heard Clyde's instructions and began to slither into the back, and then he grabbed the wobble pump handle and again began the pumping process.

During this time, the airplane gained a small amount of speed and was able to fly out of ground effect. Slowly they gained altitude and were able to make a small heading adjustment toward the Aleutian Islands.

About three hours out they were able to climb to an altitude of six thousand feet just east of the Kuril Islands. Clyde became increasingly confident in the airplane's operation and performance.

"Okay, Hugh, let's get ready to drop the gear."

He reached under the control panel and felt the small T-handle at the end of a cable. He pulled the handle and immediately heard a loud sound as the landing gear structure ripped its way out of the airplane mounting holes. It felt like they had just released a large drag chute. Airspeed began to increase as the airplane started an aggressive climb.

Both Clyde and Hugh were filled with exhilaration. "It's working!" cried Clyde. "It's working! I calculated a significant improvement in performance, and it appears we are getting everything I hoped for!"

Night had descended, and visibility was limited to just a faint source of moonlight. As the airplane climbed to fourteen thousand feet, it immediately encountered airframe icing conditions.

"Boy, could we use one of those new fangled anti-icing systems! They have them on the drawing boards right now for advanced structures but I suspect they'll never come up with anything for these cloth babies'." Clyde exclaimed. "I suspect that during this time of year, we will be plagued with ice the whole way there."

The only means to avoid ice was to reduce altitude to warmer air or to increase altitude to colder temperatures, where the water in the air was already in the form of ice before it hits the airframe and therefore will not stick. Since Clyde wasn't sure if warmer conditions existed below, the best option was to increase altitude into colder air. Further, at higher altitudes, the larger WASP engine enjoyed more optimum performance conditions.

There was one physical reason for not wanting to fly higher, however. Human beings were not made to live well at higher altitudes. Below ten thousand feet, most persons can manage fairly well, while above ten thousand feet, strange things can happen. Most people will get headaches, loose appetite, and loose mental competence. Clyde later realized that partially because of his chain smoking habit, Hugh suffered significantly from lack of oxygen and became all but useless above ten thousand feet. Clyde, on the other hand, was unusually tolerant of high altitude and seemed to thrive in these conditions.

41

Miss Veedol Reaches Altitude

Clyde flew *Miss Veedol* to seventeen thousand feet, and there he leveled off. Hugh felt he was ready to die.

"What's wrong, Hugh? You look like you're sick!" Clyde hollered.

"I'm alright. I just need a cigarette."

"The conditions are such that we'll have to fly at this altitude for some time. Can you hold out alright? You know you can't have a cigarette; in fact, I expect you might as well throw them away. You can't smoke until we get to Seattle in a couple of days. I assume you realized that before we left," Clyde told him.

"Don't worry about me, Clyde. I'll be alright. We have to make this thing work. I have no choice."

The air was clear, with outside temperatures running below zero. Inside, there was no source of direct heat. Engine cooling oil circulating through the engine ran through tanks mounted beneath each of the seats and provided some minimal warming to the touch. The tanks were covered with an insolating blanket to prevent those who sat upon them from getting burned. But the air temperature inside the airplane basically felt as cold as it was outside. Unfortunately, Clyde and Hugh had left behind most of their warm clothes and boots to save weight.

As they leveled off, Clyde began to hear an unusual whistling and banging sound below the floor—probably outside in the wind stream.

Looking out the window in the dark, sharply downward toward the earth, he could make out the outline of several strut parts of the landing gear that had not separated as planned.

"Damn, Hugh, it looks like we have a problem. We still have part of the landing gear attached to the belly. The pins were facing aft and the wind stream didn't rip them off. This could be serious. Not only will it increase drag, but upon our belly landing, the struts could spear through the floor near where we sit—a possible fatal situation."

Even at this altitude, in sub-zero temperatures, and in the dim moonlight, Clyde decided that he had to do something about the remaining gear struts protruding into the air stream below. Because of his barnstorming days, he was accustomed to operating outside of an airplane, but never had done so at these extreme conditions. He felt he had no choice but to go outside and remove the offending stucture. Without warm clothes and boots, he had little to protect him from the frigid air rushing by at one hundred ten miles per hour.

"Hugh, take over the controls and hold it as slow and steady as you can while I dispose of those pesky struts."

Within minutes he climbed out of the front port cockpit window and stepped onto the forward wing strut with one stocking-clad foot. He hung on for dear life with one hand in the ground crew D-handle. By lying down facing aft and across the two wing struts, he could reach the strut on the port side. The frigid wind blew up his pants leg and light jacket.

Figure 20. Clyde works outside of Miss Veedol at 17,000 feet in the dark at sub zero temperatures to remove remaining landing gear struts (simulated)

Luckily, the locknut and safety wire were removed in hopes of it tearing away with the main part of the gear. Using two hands, he was able to unscrew the strut from the airframe and drop it into dark void below. The starboard strut was out of reach.

He was cold—frozen beyond belief! Nonetheless, he had to make it back to the window edge, where Hugh might possibly be able to help him into the cab. With all of his energy directed to forcing an upward motion in the lateral slip stream, he reached the lower window frame with his frozen fingers and tried to yell for help.

Hugh turned loose of the controls and reached for Clyde's arm with two hands. Because no one was flying the airplane, and with all of the passenger weight shifted to the left, the airplane banked into an uncoordinated left turn. Clyde had to be lifted against the slip stream directly into the open cockpit window. Once in, Clyde fell motionless into the pilot's seat as Hugh jumped into his seat and fought the controls on the copilot side to get the airplane once again under control.

Even with no direct heater, sitting on the warmer seat and out of the direct blast of the cold air, Clyde felt like he was is heaven. He spent some time trying to thaw out and get motion back into his arms, legs, and fingers. After about twenty minutes, he was able to talk and tell Hugh about the ordeal. "In all my years as a stunt pilot, I never experienced anything as grueling as that!" he said "I would never, ever do anything like that again unless it was absolutely necessary!"

Hugh then replied, "At least you were able to get one of the struts. Maybe we will just have to take our chances and live with the other strut hanging onto the airplane."

"What are you talking about?" Clyde said sternly, "We have go to clean up the airplane completely or we're dead! We have got to finish what we set out to do!"

Before anything else could be said, Clyde swung the controls to the pilot's side, and had Hugh reposition himself. Clyde opened the copilot window and climbed out of it. Going through the same procedure outside, he was able to accomplish the strut removal in much less time, as he had learned the process required previously with the other strut. Back in the cab, total recuperation took more than two hours. To aide the warming process, Hugh reached for the hot tea to offer Clyde. When it didn't pour, Hugh discovered the tea was frozen solid.

42

Back Home

At the hospital in Boise, the little operation patient, Ellen Strasser, was making a remarkable recovery from her surgery. On the day after the operation, she was able to sit up in a chair. Diane stood in the room and watched her mother read to Ellen from one of her storybooks. It warmed her heart to realize that this child, who only a couple of days earlier had been out of breath and in deep pain, was smiling and laughing when she pointed to a picture of a bunny rabbit. When her mother looked up and saw Diane, she got up with Ellen in her arms and went to hug her.

"Can you believe how well she's doing?"

"It's a miracle," Diane said. She tickled Ellen under the chin, and the child laughed and squirmed. "Maybe we should put her back into bed. She shouldn't get too tired."

"Of course, you're right."

She placed the child back in her crib, and within minutes she was sound asleep. Then the mother sat in a chair and soon she nodded off too. Diane stayed there and watched them, almost transfixed.

Diane thought about Clyde and wondered how the flight was going. Along with the struggle of the flight itself, she knew there would be a lot of physical discomfort. But he was a strong man, and she felt confident that he would be fine. Last night she and her mother had a long talk about her future, and Diane was thinking more clearly about what she wanted and what she didn't want.

June had filled her in on the pitfalls of marriage and what it took for a marriage to succeed. One of the most important things was that a couple had to want the same things. Her mother told her that with a man like Clyde she would have to be patient. For the first time, Diane heard the story of her parents' courtship—how they met, how her father had gotten cold feet twice, and that their wedding had been postponed for over a year. Diane was shocked.

"How did you convince him to marry you?" Diane asked June.

"I didn't. I was the right woman for him. The problem was that he didn't know that, and it took time for him to come to that realization."

Diane sighed. "You and daddy were meant for each other. But I'm not sure about Clyde and me."

She was brought back to the present when the Dr. Garrison walked into the room and went to stand by Ellen's crib. The little girl was sleeping peacefully.

"You did a great job in the operating room, Diane," he said. "Have you thought of becoming a surgical nurse? You're perfectly suited to the job. I'd love to have you assist me in surgery all the time."

Diane looked up at him, not knowing what to say, but feeling prouder than she ever had in her life. "You've given me something to think about, doctor."

He checked Ellen and smiled, then nodded at Diane and left the room.

He thinks I should become a surgical nurse, Diane thought. Becoming a surgical nurse was something she dreamed of but always thought was too far out of reach. She never thought she possessed the necessary skills.

Surgical nurses were the nurses Diane admired the most. They specialized in preoperative care, meaning care provided to surgical patients before, during, and after surgery. In many instances they became closer to the patients than other nurses did. This was the part of the job Diane liked the most, especially when the patient was a child. Then it dawned on her that what she really wanted to be was a "pediatric nurse", one that would watch after children. It would mean further schooling, but if it was what she really wanted, not pursuing it would be a mistake.

She loved the excitement of surgery, which was never routine, no matter what surgeons might claim. Every surgical procedure required a great deal of preparation and work to go smoothly, whether it was a procedure that was performed on a regular basis or not.

During preoperative care, Diane always became close to her patients. And though some doctors and nurses felt keeping a distance was better all around, she didn't feel that way. Obviously, Dr. Garrison agreed with her. It just fit—it was everything she had always wanted and sought in her career—and she has a good surgeon who believes in pediatrics and who felt she was right for the job!

* * * * *

A few hours after Clyde and Hugh took off, Alice Boardman called her staff into main dining room. "I'm having company tonight, and I want everything to be perfect. First, make sure this house is sparkling clean from top to bottom," she said, addressing the maids. "Cook, polish the good silver until it gleams and use my best china. We'll be celebrating my son and everything must be perfect. I'm putting together the menu myself and will give it to you when I'm finished."

The servants scurried out of the room to attend to their duties. Later the menu for the evening meal became available; it consisted of turtle soup, lobster mousse, and lamb. The cook had only made turtle soup once before, but Alice insisted it was a delicacy and sent her off to do the grocery shopping.

The dining room glittered with crystal, lace, and silver—silver platters for the appetizers and silver bowls for the chocolate and the roses.

"Some of the pieces are almost two hundred years old," Mrs. Boardman explained to the cook and one of the maids. "The coffee pot belonged to my great-great-grandmother."

"Did they bring it from Europe?" the maid asked.

"No, this is American silver. My family has been in this country for four generations. We're American through and through."

The maid and the cook nodded at each other. "That's so different from either one of us," the cook said in a heavy Irish brogue.

"Yes, it is. But then again, people are the same everywhere." Mrs. Boardman smiled and that softened her face.

Alice wore dark blue silk for the evening and thought she looked better than she had in ages. Her hairdresser had put her silver hair into chignon, and with a subtle amount of make-up, she looked ten years younger than her fifty-seven years. This party would be the social event of the month, and she wanted Hugh to be proud of her.

Mary Ellen came with Alice and as usual had very little to say. She marveled at the attention to detail her mother in law spent on the event.

Alice's sister, Lois, arrived first. "I'm leaving for Europe in two weeks!"

Alice frowned at her, annoyed. This was Hugh's night, and she didn't intend for anyone to upstage him. "Did you know that Hugh met some of our relatives when he was in London? They took him out to brunch and were very impressed by the venture he was embarking on."

"I know, and I wish him a safe and successful journey," Lois said. "Don't you think a month in Paris and Rome is a marvelous thing? Perhaps when Hugh returns, you might want to join me!"

"I'll be spending that time with Hugh and his new wife Mary Ellen, here. Did you forget that they just got married two months ago?"

"Since I didn't get an invitation to the wedding, I…"

The arrival of other guests prevented a confrontation between the two sisters for which Alice was grateful. Once the other guests arrived, the servants moved around the table passing the silver platters, pouring ice water out of the silver pitchers, and being careful not to spill anything. Talk circled the table—not all of it about Hugh.

"The stock market crash two years ago is still having a devastating effect on many businesses," one of the guests said.

"So many small businesses are going under," Eleanor Garten said. "People are watching every dime they spend. I'm so grateful that we don't have to, but it still has an effect on us."

Suddenly, Alice lifted her glass. "I don't know how to tell you how proud we all are of Hugh. He's a remarkable young man who has set off on an adventure that will change the world."

She and Mary Ellen could hardly hold back the tears that filled their eyes. They knew they were among friends who loved Hugh as much as they did.

"Let's say a prayer for Hugh," Alice said, and they all bowed their heads.

* * * * *

In Wenatchee, Opal climbed the steps to the local mercantile. Before she went inside, she glanced up at the sky, thinking of Clyde and wondering where he was at that moment. It was a very warm day for October, but not warm enough to cause perspiration at the back of her neck. *That woman*, Opal thought. She had just gotten off the phone with Alice Boardman and had to get out of the house before she exploded.

She went to one of the tables at the back of the store and began to look through the material. Finally, she found something that she liked and bought enough to make Clyde a new shirt. After some thought, she bought twice as much so she could make one for Percy too.

At the cash register, the cashier rang up her purchases and asked her if she'd heard anything from Clyde. She laughed, knowing that he was thousands of miles away in the sky. How would that be possible? All of Wenatchee was holding its breath, waiting for him to land safely. But there was another mother whose son was up in the sky too, and Opal couldn't stand her and hoped she never had to see her again.

Alice Boardman was just about the nastiest woman Opal had ever come across. If Hugh was anything like her she pitied Clyde having to put up with him in such close quarters. Every time she talked to her she always mentioned the fact that she had put up the money for the flight and that if it hadn't been for her it wouldn't have been possible. She made Hugh sound like the more experienced pilot and came right out and said that Clyde was there to help him.

Opal walked back home. People pulled her over with questions about Clyde and the flight and were surprised to learn that she didn't know much more than they did. All of a sudden this boy, who might have been eleven or twelve years old, came up to her and started talking about aviation like he was an experienced flier.

"I want to be a wing walker just like Clyde. He's my hero."

Opal smiled down at the boy. "Would you like to come home with me? I'll show you some of Clyde's things."

"Wow! Sure I would."

When they got to her home, Opal put her purchases away and turned the radio on to see if there was any word on Clyde. Then she took the boy, whose name was Joseph, into Clyde's bedroom and watched him look wide-eyed at Clyde's things, including the awards he'd won for stunt flying and a miniature model of the first airplane he'd flown. Joseph was fascinated, and Opal thought that if Clyde knew the boy worshipped him so much he would have been embarrassed. Joseph stood there, and Opal thought it looked like he was going to cry.

"Can I touch the plane?" he asked.

"Of course you can." She handed it to him. He held it in his hands gingerly, turning it over and over, and then returned it to Opal.

"It's the greatest thing I've ever seen." Joseph said. "And this is the best day of my life."

Opal thought for a moment, then she put her hand on Joseph's arm and smiled at him. "If your parents give their permission, how would you like to be there when Clyde and Hugh land?"

"Are you kidding? I get to meet Clyde Pangborn. Wow."

"He's going to be very tired, but I'm sure he'll at least say hello to you. But you have to get your parents' permission, and I have to talk to them too. If this is something they don't want you to do, then you won't be able to."

"Sure. I better get going now. I'll ask my mom as soon as I get home."

Opal walked Joseph down the pathway. Being with him reminded her of Clyde when he was a boy—the curiosity and the need for adventure. She hoped his parents encouraged him in his endeavors. When she walked back into the house, the phone was ringing. Thinking it might be news about Clyde; she hurried to answer it and was disappointed to hear Alice Boardman's voice.

"Have you gotten any word?" Alice asked.

"I don't know any more than you do," Opal said. "I keep hoping, but so far, nothing."

"Well, if you hear anything, be sure you call me right away," Alice said. "You do have my phone number."

"You gave it to me five times, and you gave it to my son Percy twice. Yes, if I hear anything, I'll call you.'

"Just make sure you do!" Alice said and slammed the phone down.

43

The Long Journey

In the airplane, the tensions were tight but for a different reason. The en route portion of the trip could be described as the worst of all worlds. It was monotonous, a boring nightmare from which there was no escape. To begin with, it was freezing cold—sub-zero at times—and there was no way to keep warm. Their breath stuck to the inside of the windows and formed an opaque layer of frost so that visibility was either zero or next to zero. Even if they could see outside, the scene was dismal. Everything was frozen. Two windows were cracked open to maintain some level of ventilation to keep the moisture down around them. Clyde understood that ventilation was a form of leakage, which meant added drag. For this reason they used the smallest interior flow possible.

Hugh remained fairly busy pumping fuel to the upper wing tanks and transferring fuel from the five-gallon tins into the large body tanks. Most of them were gone now, but there still remained several more to go. A siphon line with a bulb starter was available to transfer the fuel into the large tanks. As Hugh slumped in the aft compartment, he would lift one tin at a time to the top of the large body tanks. Then he would open both lids and stick the siphon hose into both with the end going into the tin all the way to the bottom. The tins were modified to have the opening on one of the sides rather on the end to reduce their height. The end of the tube was cut at a slight slant so that only a small drop of fuel remained once the tank was emptied.

Once properly arranged, Hugh pumped the rubber bulb to start the flow from the tin into the tank. Depending on the smoothness of the air, he had to slouch there and stabilize the tin until it was empty. This was only one-half of the job. All of the fuel from the tins had to be hand-pumped to the upper wing tanks using the wobble pump before he was through.

When the tank emptied, he would throw an oil rag at Clyde to get his attention. Clyde would slow the airplane down to one hundred miles per hour and put it into a hard sideslip to the right. Meanwhile, Hugh unzipped the upper starboard aft window-type access. The attached portion would flap violently in the outside turbulent flow. He positioned the tin in the window, ready to throw it out, but held onto it until both were comfortable that it could be released without hitting the horizontal tail surface.

Clyde yelled out, "Go!"

That was the signal they established to let the tin loose. They both observed intently for any indication that the tin had struck the airplane. If the tin were to hit the airplane, it could dent the frame or tear the fabric on the tail. A drag increase and loss in stability or tail power might result, so it was important to follow the procedure rigorously.

Eight hours into the flight, all of the fuel was transferred into the large body tanks but not yet transferred to the upper wing tanks. They were successful in disposing of the empty tins one hundred percent of the time.

Clyde was dreaming of a steaming hot cup of coffee or a bowl of his mother's hot soup. At times he found himself thinking of Diane or Yumiko. Hugh dreamed of a warm bed with his new wife, Mary Ellen, beside him.

Hugh remarked, "I suspect Mary Ellen is living quite well at this time—probably having tea in some warm place with mother and her friends. I bet they have no idea of what we are going through—or even care for that matter."

Mostly Clyde and Hugh did their best to keep their sanity and to refrain from arguing too often. The latter was difficult to do since their tempers were short.

"Pay attention to what you're doing," Clyde said more than once.

Hugh frowned. "Maybe you're used to being bored to death. I'm not."

"Bored? There's so much to do I'm having trouble keeping it all straight, but I have to. So stop all your damn complaining!" Clyde yelled.

"I'm freezing to death," Hugh said several times.

He was right. They were not dressed for the occasion and could not even use each other for warmth. Because the space inside was so confined and the equipment storage was limited, the two were typically separated by inches but positioned shoulder to shoulder. Without shoes or boots, their feet were frozen, but they could keep blood circulating through them by rubbing them together. There was little or no reason to keep their feet on the rudder peddles as the airplane was well-trimmed. Both remained in front during most of the trip except for those times when Hugh would move to the rear to work the wobble pump transferring fuel to the upper wing tanks.

"What I need is a hot brick like the one my mother used on cold nights when there was no heat," Clyde said. "That would keep my feet nice and toasty."

"A pair of wool socks would work for me. Whose idea was this dumb flight anyway?"

Clyde glared at him. "You know damn well it was both our ideas. Damn, it's freezing in here." He tried to flex his fingers and his toes, but they were too stiff. "I'm afraid of frostbite. Try to move your toes, Hugh, it might help."

Hugh tried to move his fingers and toes the way Clyde had, but had no better luck.

"That figures," Clyde said. "Rich boys like you are too soft."

Hugh glared at him.

"I shouldn't have said that," Clyde said. "We're both cold and hungry."

Food was is short supply, and they had doled out what they had sparingly. The problem was they didn't have much. During the last-minute chaos before takeoff, Fritz apparently grabbed the wrong bag of chicken and only gave them the one containing wings and backs. The heavy meat pieces such as the breasts and legs were left in Japan. Even these bony parts were so frozen that only small pieces of meat could be removed slowly with their teeth using considerable persistence. Each piece had to be thawed out in their mouths before it could be chewed and swallowed.

Water or tea canteens were held between their legs or behind their backs to keep them from freezing. Even then, it was rationed from the start of the trip to assure that the limited supply would last throughout the planned forty hours. Minimum water was boarded as part of the weight-saving effort.

"Do you think we'll loose a few pounds?" Hugh asked. He took a tiny sip of water and closed the cap on the canteen tightly. "Know something? Water never tasted so good, especially when you pretend its gin."

"How about a vodka martini?" Clyde laughed. "No, without the olive it just doesn't work. Anyway there's a prohibition, so it's all illegal."

Hugh kept laughing. "Who's going to find us up here?" he asked. "Actually, I'm too sick to eat—all I want to do is sleep."

"That's not a good idea," Clyde said and shook him so he wouldn't nod off. "You have an important job to do."

Despite their efforts to lighten the situation, their battle with being cold and hungry was real. All the work they had to do took their minds off their discomfort, but at times it became too difficult and they took it out on each other. Clyde was aware of the fact that Hugh had always lived an easy life, but that didn't mean he wanted to listen to his constant complaints.

"Another five minutes of this and I'll open the cockpit window and jump out," Hugh said. "I want a steak sandwich and a beer."

"Take a nap and maybe you'll dream about one," Clyde said. "Then when you wake up maybe you'll be praying for having the work you have to do."

The constant ear-breaking roar of the engine made it impossible to do anything but wait for milestones, which were hours apart. The engine didn't purr; it rambled on in a continuous sequence of clangs, beats, and whirls. The two were nervous about any interruptions in this constant sequence as they knew their options were zero if anything happened to the single engine supporting them in the air.

Turning back was not even a consideration—they could only charge forward. Land was nowhere within reach even if they glide from this high altitude, should that become necessary. All survival gear, including life rafts, wet suits, and warm clothing were left behind in the interest of saving weight. Their only hope in a forced landing would be the unlikely chance of an isolated fishing vessel being near by. They could only keep sane by sleeping or keeping their minds on other things disassociated with the trip.

Sleeping was the most obvious escape for Hugh as the altitude sickness and lack of nicotine kept his mind in a stupor. Since he couldn't get enough oxygen from the air at such a high altitude, he had a headache and did not feel like eating.

He had one job—but a vital one—and that was to keep the upper fuel tanks full to keep the engine running and the airplane's center of gravity in check.

Clyde had his hands full maintaining control of the airplane attitudes and flight path. His job was overwhelming as he had little time to sleep, and his attention span was wearing thin. Often his mind would deviate to his home life and the girl he left behind. Diane would subconsciously pop into his head to encourage him to come home safely. He longed for a successful trip completion even though the finish line was yet far ahead.

Talking was impossible. Shouting was the only way of communicating unless reasonable sign language could be properly interpreted. They wore flight helmets to keep their ears warm, but these warmers further aggravated the problems with communication.

Sleeping was difficult but at the same time it presented a hazard in assuring they kept alert and aware of their responsibilities. Each had to monitor the other to assure that adverse dozing wasn't happening when he was responsible for critical piloting or navigation chores.

44

A Close Call

During one of these boring times they were both alerted to an apparent engine malfunction. The mighty engine coughed, shaking the airframe violently, as though it was tired and wanted to quit. The two pilots didn't know exactly where they were over the earth, only that they were far out in the middle of the frigid ocean.

Clyde urgently stretched out of his seat to stick his head up into the wing root area to view the glass tube fuel gauges. "We are out of fuel! Hugh, you let the wing tanks go dry!"

"Oh, God!" Hugh said.

Hugh frantically began to pump the wobble pump handle. Luckily, he was in the rear compartment close to the wobble handle when this happened. Adrenalin had set in, making him pump vigorously, but it was still very tiring and hard for Hugh at this high altitude. Finally, the engine began to show signs of recovery and pulled the Bellanca more smoothly through the air. With that, Hugh pumped for more than an hour, but it was far from adequate to fill the overhead tanks. Hand pumping over two hundred gallons by hand was no small job. Consequently, he had to pause after the wing tanks were only about half full.

"I swear this will never happen again," Hugh said as he resumed his pumping.

Clyde just breathed deeply and said nothing.

They finally were able to see their first sign of land. By scraping the frost off of a side window, they recognized it as one of the key volcanoes included in the Aleutian Chain near Altu Island. Their hearts filled with excitement as for the first time they had validation that they truly were on the predetermined great-circle course. What a thrill it was to see ground below them again. They felt a shot of adrenalin to know they were in a position where they could at least feel the love of mother earth. The frigid lashing sea viewed in all directions was depressing.

Clyde even managed a smile. "Are you as relieved as I am?"

"I would say so!" Hugh said.

"To think we're on course makes me even more determined to make this flight a success." His smile grew bigger. "We're going to make it, Hugh. I swear we will."

Within a short period of time, the elation they felt died down, and they were back to more pure, miserable boredom. They knew of the horrible weather patterns that existed in the region as they passed into the Bering Sea and were somewhat thankful for being in *Miss Veedol*'s sheltered cabin. Even though this marked a key point of progress, they still had a major part of their journey ahead of them. Together, they had to keep alert, keep the nose pointed in the right direction, and keep the engine running.

"By the way, Hugh, did you know it is yesterday? Somewhere about here we cross the International Date Line where we loose a day. It feels like we already put in a full day, and then we lost it," Clyde remarked.

"All I want to do is sleep," Hugh said and he began to nod off.

Clyde shook him. "I need you to stay awake, damn you! Stay awake. You have work to do!"

Suddenly, just as it happened before, but more abrupt, the engine completely died when Hugh was snuggled down in the front seat. Even with all his years of stunt flying, Clyde had never felt the shock of fear that he experienced at that moment. He quickly tried everything on the panel to diagnose the problem. Just then he forced his head back to where he could barely view the overhead tank fuel level gauges and again found them to read empty.

"Shit, Hugh!" he shouted, "You did it again! When did you last fill the main tanks? I thought you promised it would never happen again. What the hell are you trying to do, get us both killed?"

Hugh didn't say a thing but leaped over the tanks and frantically began operating the manual wobble pump. But exerting a great deal of work at the high altitude was just too much for him. This time, the heavy pumping activity was too late and did not aid in keeping the engine running.

"There is no way to start this engine unless we can get it to wind-mill!" Clyde hollered. "Keep pumping, but hang on, I'll have to build up our speed."

He put the airplane into a steep dive, and the speed grew... 110...120...130 miles per hour. The flat prop pitch set on the ground to enhance the takeoff performance was acting against them. Wind milling the engine would require a much faster speed because of this pitch. Before long, the airplane would be approaching its maximum design speed where calculations showed that the aerodynamic forces might start tearing the fabric or breaking some of the wooden structure. No one really knew what would happen above this speed as that type of dangerous testing has been avoided.

"We are going to get this prop turning or die trying!" Clyde shouted with absolute terror in his eyes.

Hugh just pumped, equally terrified, as he could see the end of his life rapidly approaching.

There was still no engine response. Clyde pushed the nose over fur-ther...140...150...160 miles per hour.

"Spin, damn it, spin!" Clyde shouted.

Hugh did nothing but pump the wobble handle. He could not look out as his concentration on his job wouldn't allow it. But inside he was praying for life in that big radial engine up front. He was filled with more guilt than he had ever experienced in his life.

The plane began to shake. Along with the terrific wind noise, the windows and much of the interior began to buffet violently. Minor inte-rior pieces were beginning to break, and their parts were flying around the cab. The breaking sounds were minor as the airframe still seemed to be holding its integrity. But, still no prop response. The cold icy waters were coming up rapidly.

"I won't die this way," Hugh thought.

Clyde, as usual, was all action.

"I pray this baby holds together!" he shouted. "We'll have to squeeze every ounce of strength out of her! Hold together, hold together, now. Of all times I am hoping the *Pangborn Factor* will pull us through. Keep pumping, Hugh, keep pumping! Shit! That water is coming up fast. Come on! Turn, damn it!"

He pushed the nose over so that it seemed that the airplane was now heading straight down. Finally at one hundred eighty miles per hour—some twenty miles an hour over placard speed—the propeller jerked a partial rotation, then another, and another, and shortly thereafter the engine came to life. Clyde quickly throttled back to prevent the engine from over-speeding and to prevent more build-up in airplane speed.

Clyde had to arrest the altitude loss before they crashed into the sea. He pulled hard on the yoke with both hands so that their bodies were forced down hard against the bottom of their seats. Joe told Clyde at the Bellanca Company to never combine excessive speed with excessive pull-out loads but he had no choice. The forces were so high that Hugh found it impossible to continue his fuel-pumping effort. There was fear that the high speed in combination with the pullout loads would rip the wings off *Miss Veedol* as she continued to fly well beyond her design flight limits.

Finally, the nose lifted above the horizon, and the airplane began a slow deceleration toward normal flying conditions.

"We are at fourteen hundred feet!" cried Clyde. "If we continued our dive for another five seconds, we would have become fish food."

"Hugh," Clyde said, "What the shit were you doing? Get with it! As I explained to you before, you have one primary job other than spelling me off to rest! You have been completely useless on this trip. If it weren't for the need of occasional rest, I could have done better by myself. That one almost cost us our lives! In all my daredevil life, I've never been so scared of coming out alive than I was that time… You idiot!" He looked over at Hugh and Hugh was curled into the pre-natal position, crying and shaking from head to toe. "What's wrong with you, Hugh. Shake it off, get up and start pumping—hard!"

"My mother must be driving everyone nuts," Hugh mumbled.

"Your mother, is that what you're thinking about? You have got to get more serious about this trip right here, right now and get your mind off of those things back home, or you will never see back home again. We still have a lot further to go, so shape up!"

Climbing back to fourteen thousand feet, they again entered the realm of severe boredom.

"You have got to set up some sort of a schedule, Hugh. We cannot afford another one of those! Get in back and pump until I tell you to stop. You cannot rest in your seat up here until both of those tanks are full, do you hear me?"

The only word of their progress during the whole flight came from a small Aleutian island where an amateur operator radioed America that he had heard an airplane passing over above the clouds.

No one was even sure of their final destination, though Clyde's mother was adamant that her son would choose her home in Wenatchee, Washington, as his landing site. She was among thirty locals, news reporters, and other enthusiasts who maintained a vigil at its little airfield carved out of the sagebrush near the Columbia River.

45

Opal and Alice Boardman Meet

Meanwhile in the Wenatchee post office, Opal waited patiently for her mail. She amused herself by looking at the dust motes in the shaft of sunlight, all the while her mind was on Clyde. The air inside was chilly and smelled of wood and glue.

"Autumn is definitely here," Sara, the postmistress, said. She said that to everyone who came in that day. It was a nice, safe thing to say.

"It's my favorite time of year," Opal said as she looked through the mail. Most of the cards were for Clyde from well-wishers.

"You must be very excited," Sara said. "Tonight's the night, isn't it?"

Opal swallowed hard. "No, tomorrow morning at seven, they'll land at seven here in Wenatchee."

"But, I thought… Mrs. Reed was in today with her boy Joseph, and they told me he's going to be there with you. She seemed certain it was going to be earlier."

"No, if I know Clyde, and I do, it will be seven in the morning when they land."

The postmistress smiled. "Well, give him my best when you see him. We're all praying for him."

Opal put the mail in her handbag and turned to go. Just then the door flew open, admitting a burst of cool October air. Opal's heart almost stopped beating as she gazed at the tall woman standing in the middle of the doorway.

It was Alice Boardman, resplendent in a mink coat and a big diamond ring on her hand. What was she doing here? Opal had never met her before, and she despised her on sight. She looked exactly the way Clyde had described her: a rich snob. And she looked totally out of place in the tiny Wenatchee post office. Even Sara stared at her.

"Mrs. Boardman?" Opal said, extending her hand. "My goodness, what are you doing here?"

Alice shook Opal's hand limply, and Opal disliked her even more. As a girl Opal's father had taught her that a firm handshake showed good character and a limp one showed no character.

"Your son, Percy, told me you would be here," Alice Boardman said. "I thought perhaps I could take you to lunch and we could get to know each other."

"That sounds nice. There's a nice diner down the street we could go to."

"No, no," Alice said, almost as if she might be poisoned at a diner in Wenatchee. "I thought we'd take a nice drive toward Spokane and eat there."

"Well, there is a nice place between here and Spokane that Clyde patronizes. He says they serve the best steak. We don't have much time, though."

Alice smiled. "It's noon now, we'll be back by four o'clock. I just thought that since our sons will soon be world-famous that we should get to know each other. Don't you agree?"

Opal thought she might be right, but still felt uneasy as they climbed into the backseat of Alice's car. It wasn't until she took a better look that she realized there was a chauffeur sitting in the front seat. *Rich people certainly know how to live,* Opal thought.

"Beautiful car," Opal said, searching for something to say.

"I only bought it a few weeks ago. It's a Packard and has all the amenities you can think of."

"I have a Ford Model T that's almost seven years old, but I don't travel much anymore. In the early days, we had to travel by horseback. Did Clyde ever tell you about that?"

Alice shook her head. "No, he never did, but that must have been just awful. How did you bathe and wash clothes?"

Opal looked at the floor almost not knowing how to answer. Obviously, this woman had never struggled for anything in her life. She almost felt sorry for her because she probably had no idea how much pride there could be in a hard day's work. If she was like this, then perhaps her son was too. She said a silent prayer for Clyde.

"We washed our clothes in creeks and rivers and bathed there too as often as we could. No, it wasn't easy, but my husband and I and our sons were never closer. For Clyde and Percy it was a big adventure."

There was a buzzing in Opal's ear, the force of her own blood pumping in her head, she reasoned. Alice droned on and on about Hugh and what a great pilot he had become and what a big help to Clyde he had to be. How could she say such ridiculous things? If they came home safely, it would be because of Clyde's skill as an aviator, not because of some spoiled rich boy who might become a part of history because of his family's money. Clyde had struggled and worked hard his whole life to get to this point. No one was going to ruin it for him.

Suddenly Opal realized it made no difference what Alice said. She could talk all she wanted and it changed nothing. All she wanted to do was get away from her, skip the so-called friendly lunch and never catch sight of that red lipstick again. Alice Boardman was made up like a young woman in her twenties, and Opal thought she looked like she was trying to be much younger and suddenly felt pity for her.

Alice's behavior puzzled Opal. The last time they had spoken on the phone they had said good-bye on such bad terms that she hoped they would never speak to each other again. Now here they were socializing together, which seemed odd to Opal since she disliked Alice and was certain Alice felt the same way. So, what did Alice want from her?

She turned away abruptly and looked out the car window, hoping Alice would stop talking about all of Hugh's accomplishments. Clyde had told her that Hugh's greatest accomplishment was probably the number of women he dated at one time.

In less than two hours they found the restaurant easily. They hurried down the steps and walked inside where they were met by the hostess who handed them two menus and showed them to a table.

"This is a very nice place," Alice said. "Have you been here before?"

"No, but Clyde, Percy, and his wife have been. With the amount of traveling Clyde does, I have no idea how many different restaurants he's been to."

Alice examined the menu. "The clams casino looks good. Why don't we start with that?"

"Sure," Opal said. She had no idea what clams casino were. "You do the ordering. You have more experience with such things."

Alice smiled, and Opal knew she'd made her happy. Alice ordered chicken cacciatore for both of them, and that surprised Opal since she'd expected something like pheasant-under-glass. Alice also ordered a bottle of white wine. Opal was careful not to drink much because Clyde and Percy had always told her she got drunk easily.

"I'm enjoying the meal, but I hate being away from the radio in case there's news," Opal said.

Alice motioned for the waiter to come to their table. "Can you find out if there's any news about our sons?" she asked.

"Of course," the waiter said and bowed. "Mrs. Pangborn, Mrs. Boardman, I'll see what I can find out."

A few minutes later he returned with no news.

"I know Hugh will make certain they return safely," Mrs. Boardman said. She raised her glass. "To Hugh, my wonderful son."

Opal was furious, angrier than she had ever been. "How dare you!" she said. "How dare you ignore Clyde and act as though Hugh will be the one to make the flight a success. If they don't survive, it will be because of Hugh, and if they do survive, it will be because of Clyde's skill as a pilot. Your son is spoiled rich boy who has always had everything handed to him!"

"I didn't take you out to lunch to be insulted," Alice said.

Opal was surprised by how out of character she had behaved. It was rare for her to loose her temper, but she couldn't stand the way Alice ignored Clyde's contribution to the endeavor. Whatever Hugh had contributed, Clyde had contributed far more. She stopped herself, knowing that Alice was as worried about Hugh as she was about Clyde. She reached across the table and took Alice's hand.

"I know you're as worried about your boy as I am about mine. We have to believe they're going to be fine. Neither one of them would want us to think any other way."

Alice smiled, but Opal saw that her smile was insincere.

46

Diane's Truth Comes Out

The white clapboard church loomed in Diane's windshield, the arrow on the church's marquee pointing west for no reason. Her parents were religious and attended church every Sunday and believed in the Bible, but there were times when she questioned the existence of God. If people had known this, they would have been shocked, so she kept these thoughts to herself. She never told anyone, not even her parents. She drove past the church and on towards the hospital.

In less than a mile, she arrived at the hospital, got out of the car and walked into the entryway. Working in the hospital and seeing so much suffering caused her to wonder if God was real. Last night, a twenty-two-year-old man who had recently gotten engaged had died on the operating table during surgery. Two days earlier he hadn't even known he was ill, but during a basketball game he had collapsed on the court and been rushed to the hospital. Now he was dead, and his fiancée was still in the waiting room, where she had been for the last several hours, staring stone faced at her engagement ring. She had yet to shed a tear. Several times Diane had tried to speak to her, to comfort her, but she never said a word.

A young man was dead, and another man was up in the sky, and she couldn't help wondering if he would live or die. Every other thought she had was of Clyde. She wasn't in love with him, but she cared for him very, very much and would be crushed if he didn't come back safely.

When she thought of Clyde she wanted so much to believe in God and his mercy.

Once her shift was over she left the hospital quickly and drove back to the farm but found no one there. Her Brother Mike was at work, but she wondered where her parents were. Suddenly she remembered that this was the day her mother had planned to go antiquing—something she loved but rarely got to do—so she had dragged Diane's father with her.

As much as Diane loved her work, the eight-hour days were long. Knowing she would be up all night waiting for news about Clyde, she wanted to take a nap. Just as she was about to go upstairs, she heard a knock on the door and found a stranger standing there.

"Are you Diane Bronson?" the woman asked.

"Yes, I am. Who are you?"

I'm Lucy Parks from the *Boise Register*. I'm hoping you'll answer a few questions. I know our readers would love to know about your relationship with Clyde Pangborn. Is it true that you're planning to announce your engagement as soon as he lands safely?"

Diane was shocked. Where had she gotten this information? "No, that's not true. I really don't have time for any more questions."

Diane began to close the door, but the reporter held it open with her foot.

"I won't take up much of your time," Lucy said. "When did you and Pangborn meet? When will you be getting married?"

Diane was even-tempered and rarely got angry, but this woman was making her furious by intruding into her personal life. Despite this, she forced a wry laugh, touched her brow, and stepped inside the house.

"I don't know why my life is of any interest to you or anyone else in Boise," Diane said. "I'm a nurse, for heaven's sake, and I'm standing here wasting my time with you."

"Clyde Pangborn is a hero—the man of the moment. You and he are like Charles Lindbergh and Anne Morrow."

"We are not!" Diane snapped. "I'm not the daughter of a millionaire, I'm the daughter of a farmer, and Clyde and I aren't getting married— ever. We're friends and nothing more."

By the look on Lucy Parks's face, Diane knew the reporter had grown disinterested. "Then, there's nothing between the two of you."

"Yes, there is, but not what you're looking for."

Lucy turned on her heels, walked out the door and into her car. As she drove away, Diane slammed the door closed and experienced a sudden sinking feeling in the pit of her stomach. Her questions about Clyde had been answered and she was the one who had answered them. No marriage lay ahead for them, no wedding, no future. Before her meeting with Lucy Park she had wondered, but now she knew she didn't want to be Diane Bronson Pangborn. She wanted to be just plain Diane Bronson and have a private life that wasn't everyone else's business. Someday she would marry and have children, and she and her family would live an ordinary life because that was what appealed to her. She didn't want to read her name in the newspaper or have people gossip about her.

Still, she was anxious to see Clyde again and wondered where he was. A few minutes later her mother and father walked in the front door with several boxes in their arms.

"Wait till you see the beautiful blue willow serving dish I found," June said. "I couldn't resist it."

Steve placed the large package on the dining room table and carefully undid the wrapping to reveal the most intricately designed blue serving bowl Diane had ever seen.

"Your father was afraid he'd have to mortgage the farm," June said. "Weren't you, dear?" She kissed his cheek then turned to her daughter. "It's worth every penny, isn't it? Think of how wonderful it will look in the china closet."

"Did you buy it as a show piece, or do you plan to use it?" Diane asked.

"We'll use it on special occasions," June said.

"Has there been any news about Clyde?" Steve asked.

"I have not had a chance to listen to the radio, so I don't know. A reporter from the *Boise Register* was here a few minutes ago to interview me? Can you imagine? She thought that Clyde and I were engaged! We've only been out on a few dates and certainly aren't ready to get married."

Her parents were staring at her, and Diane realized that they had been wondering the same thing.

"Can you blame us?" June asked. "I've never seen you act this way over anyone else you've dated. You're completely smitten with Clyde Pangborn."

183

"No, I'm not."

Steve and June looked at her and smiled, and then Steve turned the radio on. The three of them sat on the couch and waited for news about Clyde's flight.

47

The Arrival

In the airplane, the two aviators continued to struggle. They traveled across the Gulf of Alaska just off of the rugged coastline. It was cold and offered them nothing but marginal flying weather. Violent winds coming from the Gulf continually tried to force them off course. As they approached southeast Alaska, which is famous for its bad weather, the real challenge of their navigational skills arose. Moisture blowing off the Gulf was immediately greeted by the towering eighteen-thousand-foot St. Elias Range, resulting in record rainfall and poor visibility. For hours, Clyde fought the conditions while he drove *Miss Veedol* southeast toward the Pacific Northwest.

Eventually, Clyde sighted the tip of the Queen Charlotte Islands in the moonlight off the western coast of Canada and knew the worst of the navigation nightmare was over. Clyde had been at the controls for more than thirty hours. During those long hours he tried hard not to become too annoyed with Hugh, who had slept much of the time, but it was difficult. Twice already his poor aviation skills had almost cost them their lives. Clyde had the feeling that after they landed he and Hugh wouldn't have much to do with each other. If he was honest with himself, he would admit that he resented that the flight would have been impossible without Mrs. Boardman's money. For now, though, he had other things on his mind. Aware that the tricky job of belly landing lay not too far ahead of them, he decided to catch a few hours of sleep.

"Hugh, wake up. I think we are out of the worst of it at this point. If you can take over, I'll get a chance to get some rest. Our planned belly landing is not too far ahead, and I need to be as keen as possible for that tricky maneuver."

Hugh stretched and replied, "Sure, I can do that, the long Alaska flight gave me a chance to get caught up on my sleep, so I actually feel pretty good."

"That's terrific, really great," Clyde said sarcastically.

Hugh poked him in the ribs. "Nice to see you so happy for me."

"Cut the shit," Clyde said. "Just take this heading and altitude down the coast. It will still be dark when we get there, so just watch for the city lights below on the left side of the airplane. We should be passing over Vancouver, British Columbia, in Canada in about three hours. Seattle is next, about one hour later. Wake me up when you first see the lights."

"Don't worry, I will," Hugh said.

Clyde was able to snuggle down in his seat and immediately fall asleep. Hugh did not experience too much instrument flying as the airplane traveled well above a solid layer of clouds. As he approached the northwest, the cloud layer dissipated for a while and then built up to where Hugh had to fly the heading under zero visibility conditions.

* * * * *

Later, Pangborn awoke with a start. As they broke out of the clouds, immediately ahead of them loomed the top of Mount Rainier.

"Hugh," he shouted, "Hard left, hard left! We should be slightly above the top, but with this poor lighting and barometric pressure changes, we can't be too sure. Why are we so far west in line with Mount Rainier?" He grabbed the controls. "You were supposed to wake me once we saw the city lights."

"I didn't see any lights," Hugh replied. "Maybe the cloud layer below us was too thick!"

"Look at your watch, for Christ sake. Its been five and one half hours. That should tell you something. According to the map," Clyde pointed out, "you must be way off course to find yourself over here by Mount Rainier! You are a long way west of our planned track and nearly one hundred miles south of Seattle."

Hugh frowned.

"How much fuel do we have remaining? Are we getting critical?" Clyde asked.

"I'd guess about two hundred gallons," Hugh replied.

"With that much fuel we might just continue on to Boise. If we land there, we can claim not only the first Pacific crossing but the non-stop range record as well. That would also put us in position to claim the Colonel Easterwood 'one-stop from Japan' prize to Texas." Clyde thought *Also, to land in Diane's backyard would be a real plus.* "Let's give it a try," he said to Hugh.

Clyde was disappointed that there was no way for him to get in touch with Diane. Many times during the flight he had thought of her and wondered if she was thinking of him. He wanted to see her and would as soon as he could.

He skimmed around the top of Mount Rainier and headed southeast in the direction of Boise and made a heading direct there. He thought about *how surprised Diane would be to see him and wondered what they would say to each other. After the excitement of the homecoming was over maybe they would go away someplace by themselves for a few days.* For now he had to stop thinking about her and turn his attention back to the task at hand.

Clyde was determined to make aviation history beyond the major milestone he just accomplished. Hugh would just be satisfied to land this baby and walk away alive—but Clyde had other aspirations. He knew that he had gone through a lot to get to this point, and nothing could stop him now.

As they traveled southeast, the weather deteriorated rapidly. It wasn't known if they were traveling through clouds or if the poor visibility went all the way to the ground. There was no way that they could descend to explore the bottom of the overcast as in this region the ground might come up to meet them. They had but one choice, and that was to continue on at a high altitude.

Clyde was determined. He had come a long way to grasp these records—he could not let them out of his hand now at the last minute. Soon they might run out of gas, and that would make up their minds for them.

* * * * *

187

Meanwhile, way back on the ground in Wenatchee, the small group of thirty or so people waited through the night in cold morning air. The visibility was okay, but they could see fog banks all around the area. It was well below freezing, and a light wind was blowing out of the east. Clyde's mother and brother had been there for two days now. They were encouraged to hear reports of an airplane being heard over the Aleutian Islands and later over Seattle. The report came from Seattle at about 3:00 a.m. Because of the delay in getting out the word, the actual crossing was probably closer to 2:30 a.m.

Clyde's mother had already made up her mind. Over the years, Clyde had always landed in Wenatchee at 7:00 a.m., and this time would be no different. She therefore announced to her friends in the crowd that she was going to her car to sleep and not to disturb her until 7:00.

At about 5:00 p.m. the evening before, she collected Joseph, whose parents, she suspected, would have loved to come themselves. He was about as excited as any boy could be and found it impossible to stay still even as Opal dozed off.

"I brought some comic books for you," Opal said. "Why don't you read them while I try to sleep? It's been a long day for me, and I need to get a little rest."

"Are the comics about Clyde?"

"No. I guess they are about Superman."

"Wow!" Joseph said and buried his face in the comics before dropping off to sleep.

Opal lay back in the seat wishing things could stay as simple as they were in childhood. She listened to the crowd outside calling Clyde's name and whistling and just making a racket. She knew some of them were drunk and that Clyde would disapprove since he hated drunkenness. All she wanted to do was see that her son was well, hug him, and feed him some of her home cooking, which she knew he had missed.

She dozed for a moment and dreamed that *Miss Veedol* had landed safely with Clyde alone in the plane. When she asked him where Hugh was he replied that he'd married a French women and decided to move to France. When Alice Boardman was given the news she punched Clyde in the face and broke his nose. All the onlookers were laughing at Clyde's bloody nose.

It was October 5. She awoke in the early morning and found Joseph absorbed in the comics. The dream had reminded her that Alice

Boardman would soon arrive. Opal dreaded seeing that woman again but knew that she had as much right to see her son arrive safely as Opal.

Opal dozed for a few minutes only to be awakened by a taping on the window. It was Alice. She opened the car door and Alice looked long and hard at Joseph.

"Your grandson?" she asked.

"No, just a good friend who's anxious to meet Clyde." Opal smiled at him. "Right, Joe?"

"Right!" he said and went back to his comic.

Alice smirked a little, and Opal figured she didn't like children. That figured. She tried to sleep some more, but Alice kept talking, mostly bragging about Hugh.

"I knew he would do something great some day," Alice said. "He was always trying something new, something adventurous, even as a boy. I was always so worried about him. He's still young, so this is only the beginning. Anything is possible after this."

"As long as Clyde is with him, he will be able to do anything."

"What's that supposed to mean?"

"Do you really think Hugh could have accomplished this flight on his own? Clyde could have, but Hugh? I doubt it."

"Are you insulting my son?" Alice asked with venom in her eyes.

Opal sighed. There was no point in arguing with the woman. Soon Clyde and Hugh would be here, and everything would go back to normal. Hopefully she would never have to see Alice Boardman again.

"Please excuse me, I don't mean anything. I'm just tired and worried. You must understand," Opal said as she made herself comfortable.

"Of course, how much longer will we have to wait?"

"They'll be here at 7:00. We have several hours yet."

* * * * *

The rest of the crowd was not as convinced. After all, the folks gathered had calculated that if *Miss Veedol* passed over Seattle at around 2:30 a.m., Wenatchee would only be a one-hour flight, meaning he should have been there by now. So they waited, listened, and searched the skies. It was soon 5:00 and no word, then 6:00 and no word. The crowd became nervous, and some people talked of opening up an all-points search. The apparent leaders of the group considered waking his mother and breaking the word to her that her son was obviously lost.

Finally 6:30 arrived—at least four hours after the airplane was heard over Seattle. The crowd was convinced that something bad had happened and that they must wake his mother and bring her the alarming news. Three of the onlookers were elected to do so, and they approached the car with extreme grief.

One tapped on the window as another silently practiced the words he would use to break the word. Through the window, you could see Opal stirring. As she opened the window, she exclaimed, "I beg your pardon. It's not seven yet."

The man was quick to say that he thought it was only appropriate to tell her that it had now been four hours since the airplane had been heard over Seattle and that all weather sources in the entire area, except here, state their areas are closed in.

Clyde's mother was quick to say, "Well it's not a surprise, he still has fifteen minutes before we can consider him late. If you don't mind, I still can get in a few more winks before I get up."

The three backed away, shaking their heads, only to hear someone shout, "Hey, I hear a motor off in the distance!"

Immediately others responded, "That's just another car working its way up the dirt road to the airport."

The morning was ripe with the feeling that winter was on its way, the air cool and crisp. People gathered in groups and chatted amongst themselves, trying to guess when the plane would land and if it would land safely. Opal tried to sleep but couldn't because of the noise.

At the airstrip, members of the crowd watched with wonderment. Even Opal was filled with awe, knowing what her son might have accomplished, and Joseph couldn't stop hoping up and down. Alice Boardman seemed more bored than anything else.

"Can't you keep that boy still, Mrs. Pangborn? Honestly, I have a splitting headache, and he's making it worse."

"He's excited, that's all. Everyone here is. My goodness, you certainly are a stick-in-the-mud."

Alice glared at her. "I'm a what?"

A few minutes passed when another said, "Do you hear it?" as they searched the northern sky for visual evidence. There was nothing, not a sign.

Finally, they spotted a small black dot against the white sky to the southeast.

"There they are!"

"No, that can't be them. That's probably a bird—it's in the wrong direction. They would be coming in from the north."

"The sound is coming from that direction, it may be them."

As it turned out, *Miss Veedol* aborted her determination to reach Boise. The weather was bad, and continuing on was strictly a hazard. Clyde wasn't about to take the risk. Reluctantly, he had turned the flight path around and headed for safer grounds.

48

The Landing

Many of the words being spread on the ground were echoed inside the airplane, "There it is—and there appears to be enough people there that we can catch a ride to town. You will have to climb in back for balance, Hugh. We burned all of the fuel from the floor-mounted tank, which is located behind the airplane's aerodynamic center. Now that we have burned up that aft fuel, I need your weight at the rear to give me all of the nose-up pitching moment I can get. With that help, I should be able to get the landing speed down pretty close to stall."

So Hugh, taking the path over the fuel tank that he was now well accustomed to, crawled into the back area as far as he could and strapped himself to the backside of the partition structure.

At this time, Clyde's mother emerged from her automobile to witness the excitement.

Inside *Miss Veedol*, Clyde turned to Hugh. "I assume we still have some fuel left, Hugh. You'll need to dump it before touchdown. It would be hell to be successful only to burn up after landing. Can you reach the dump lever from back there?"

"Yes, but just barely. I can loosen this strap just a bit to reach it and then tighten it back up again."

"Okay!" Clyde exclaimed, "We are about to make our final test. Can we survive a crash landing right in our own backyard? Hopefully I am awake and alert enough to bring us in and the *Pangborn Factor* holds the airframe together so that we can walk away from this alive. Now, Hugh, follow my instructions carefully. Dump the fuel when I say the word once I get on final."

As Clyde entered the base leg, he grabbed a towel, wrapped it across his forehead, and tied it around the back of his head rest.

"I expect a hard landing. Hopefully this will protect my head and neck if we come to an abrupt stop. Be sure your head is supported, Hugh."

As he turned on final approach, Clyde chopped the throttle and turned off the gas and ignition. And the large prop stopped in a horizontal position just as he had hoped.

"Okay, Hugh, DUMP! Get ready for a rough landing!"

Hugh reached out, grabbed the dump lever, and pulled it to the open position. Then he repositioned himself behind the body structure and tied himself against it using his belt and some straps used earlier to tie down the loose fuel tins that were there during the early part of the flight.

Figure 21. Miss Veedol on approach to belly landing a t Wenatchee (simulated)

Miss Veedol became an unpowered glider. With her large wing and light weight, she slowed, and Clyde skillfully pulled the nose up, approaching stall.

Just then, for some unknown reason, the propeller cranked a quarter of a turn so that it now was located in a vertical position.

"Shit!" Clyde exclaimed. "Expect to flip once that propeller digs in. I'll try to keep it out of the dirt as long as I can!"

Except for the propeller, everything else went as planned. The landing was spotted on the dirt strip exactly where Clyde had expected. The tail dragged only briefly as the airframe vibrated violently. Then there was no further nose-up rotation available, so there was nothing Clyde could do but prepare himself for the worst.

The tail hit first, creating a great cloud of dust outside and inside of the airplane. The speed was down, and the airplane decelerated a bit before the prop dug into the loose sagebrush sand. The airplane pitched down, and the speed decreased to zero almost immediately. As the prop dug in, the airplane dove to almost a vertical position, but then it flopped down on its belly and tipped onto its left wing tip.

The acceleration and deceleration forces inside were horrific. It was a God-send that Clyde had prepared himself by tying his head up tight with the towel. The rest of his body was well secured by the belt system installed in the airplane. Hugh, being snuggled up against the back-side of the structure was well protected, provided he kept his head tight against the support when they hit.

Once the airplane came to rest, there was no fire, but the interior filled with dust from the primitive landing spot. Both men were dazed and stunned. They both sat in place for a few moments as they collected their thoughts and checked themselves over for any surprising injuries.

The airplane was in an awkward position, with the pilot's side down and the copilot's window up high above Clyde. It was easy for Clyde to get unbuckled as he rested against the sidewall on the left-hand side of the cab.

Soon, Hugh let out a scream. "We made it! We made it! Clyde, are you okay?"

Hugh untied himself and proceeded to exit the rear compartment over the body fuel tanks. His head was just poking into the front cabin to where he could see that Clyde was unbuckled and getting into a more comfortable position.

Clyde immediately formed a fist and swung it at Hugh's face as hard as the cabin size constraints would allow. His early days in the rough logging camp in Idaho taught him how to punch without severely injuring his own hand.

Hugh fell back into the rear compartment, bleeding profusely over the right eye. He quickly grabbed an oil rag and placed it over his cut to help stop the bleeding.

"Clyde!" he shouted. "What are you doing? What was that all about?"

"I've wanted to do that at least a dozen times during our trip in hopes of getting your attention. This was my first opportunity to do it without jeopardizing our mission—we are two lucky guys just to be here alive!"

"But, all of those people out there, what am I going to tell them?"

"You can tell them anything you want to say, buddy."

49

Outside of the Crash Scene

Among the small gathering at the airfield was a young man, Carl Cleveland. He was just starting his career as a reporter and was employed by the local *Wenatchee Daily World*. He came up to the field three days earlier with many of the other people in hopes of getting a world scoop. He brought an assistant with him, who he placed by the only pay phone in the area.

He told his assistant, "Your job is to stay here and block this phone. If I need it in a hurry, we need to have it available instantly. Remember; keep this phone completely under your control. Here is a roll of pennies to plug into the thing if anybody comes around to use it."

Carl rushed up to the airplane to witness the events immediately as they unfolded. First to exit, live and well, was Clyde Pangborn, who immediately grabbed his mother and gave her a big hug. Her first words were, "Welcome home, son—

Figure 22. Miss Veedol smashed in the sagebrush after arrival

boy you need a bath, you stink!" A mother is the only person who could say that.

Figure 23. Hugh and Clyde outside of airplane after landing

Clyde then shook hands with his brother, turned, and took one look at the airplane. All that he could say was, "Shit." He then stood beside the airplane to address questions from the crowd.

Second and last to exit was Hugh Herndon who looked well but seemed to be protecting a cut over his right eye. He hugged his mother and then stood beside Clyde to address questions. Both said they were extremely tired and would limit their time at that location.

When asked about the trip, both agreed it was long, boring, and uncomfortable. When asked about the landing, both agreed it was truly a climax of an eventful trip. Hugh claimed all went as planned except that he was hit above the eye by a flying oil can during touchdown—but would recover.

Carl Cleveland's efforts paid off.

He was able to call his home office in Wenatchee, "PANGBORN-HERNDON SPAN THE PACIFIC. 'Boy are we glad to get here!' Pangborn puts it... 'It's like a dream come true.'"

Cleveland passed these words onto his editor in Wenatchee, who forwarded them onto the wire services, which in turn broadcasted them to the entire continent and eventually the world.

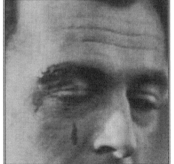

Figure 24. Hugh's right eye after being "hit by a flying oil can" during landing

50

Back at the Bellanca Airplane Company

Word quickly spread to the Bellanca Airplane Company in Wilmington, Delaware. Joe Ruggerio was just coming out of his conference room when his secretary ran up to him and broke the news.

"I can't believe it!" he exclaimed. "I didn't think it was possible!"

He immediately ran down the hall to Giuseppe Bellanca's office to tell him the good news. Giuseppe met him at the doorway and shouted the same news.

"They made it, they made it!" Giuseppe shouted as they both embraced one another. "I always knew they would—after all, they were flying the best airplane in the world. What all did they do to fly such an astoundingly distance?"

"Well," Joe said, "I am sure it took lots of luck, but a failure would have been disastrous. Guts, lots of guts! They left all of their warm clothes behind, their safety gear, and minimized even their food and drink. Most of all, they got rid of their landing gear. How they got a system that would do that past Japanese inspection is beyond me."

"Well, the important thing is that they are home and safe," Giuseppe said. "They made aviation history with our airplane and should be famous forever. What do you suppose is planned for them?"

Joe replied, "That hasn't been completely anchored down yet, as I understand it. There will be an outdoor public recognition tomorrow and a small ticker-tape parade afterward.

In the meantime, the airplane will be on display at the Bon while we prepare the parts needed and get them shipped to Seattle. Once the airplane is fixed, the two flyers will take it to New York to complete their initially planned trip around-the-world."

"We here need to do two things," Giuseppe said. "First, let's get an announcement together to share the good news with all of our employees. They have been personally involved with this thing now for months. Second, we need to invite Clyde Pangborn here to congratulate him and thank him on behalf of our company."

"I suspect he will be one busy guy for a while," Joe said. "But I will get right on that. Congratulations, sir, I am sure you are proud."

51

Their Escape

After his mother and brother hugged him again, Clyde was amazed to discover that a representative of *Asahi Shimbun* newspaper was there to present a check for twenty-five thousand dollars. It was made out to Hugh's mother, as she was listed as the sponsor of the flight. Opal and Clyde looked at each other. Opal could tell that he was angry. With Mrs. Boardman having the money, there is a good chance that Clyde's hard work in breaking the record could go unrecognized—but this was not the time to discuss it.

Then Opal turned and saw Joseph and realized that in the excitement she had almost forgotten he was there. Before she spoke, Clyde leaned down and shook the boy's hand.

Opal introduced them. "Clyde Pangborn, Joseph Reed."

"Wow," the boy said. "It's really you. When I grow up I want to be a flier just like you."

Clyde smiled and tousled the boy's hair. "You need to be prepared for a lot of hard work, then."

"Oh, I am."

Opal looked at her son. "You're exhausted, and you need to get some sleep."

The single-lane sagebrush road leading up to the landing site from town was clogged. Everyone in town was trying to come up the hill to witness the event. Luckily, this was Percy's long-time hunting grounds.

He was most familiar with the area and knew all of the back routes down the hill. He piled Clyde, Hugh, their mothers, and Joseph in his car and vanished from the scene.

Downtown, Percy arranged for secret private quarters and a full meal. Although a good relationship did not exist between Hugh and Clyde, they ate and discussed the trip before heading off for a much needed rest. During dinner, Hugh said, "Remember, Clyde, you are not to tell anyone about the flight or our experiences."

Clyde quickly responded. "What? What does that mean?"

"It was in one of those agreements that you signed before we left. You cannot tell anyone about the trip, endorse any product, or write any articles about the trip for a period of one year from now."

"You're shitting me. I'd never agree to any crap like that!" Clyde stated tersely.

"I have it in writing! You best go to sleep for now, and we will talk about the details in the morning—just remember—I'll be the spokesman for the record."

Clyde was not only disappointed but furious about why his past friend and flying companion would deceive him and treat him like this!

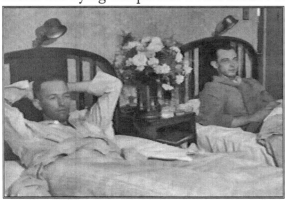

Figure 25. Clyde and Hugh rest in Wenatchee hotel following arrival

He had done his best to help this bumbling wannbe aviator, and if left to Hugh's own skills they might have been lost somewhere over the Pacific!

"I can't believe this but will wait until tomorrow to pursue it further. Right now I am going to bed—for a long, long time."

A short time later, as he laid there extremely exhausted, Clyde's mind was spinning with questions keeping him from falling instantly asleep. *What does Hugh have to gain by even writing this sort of bullshit down on paper? Does he want to claim recognition as being the one responsible for pulling off this record flight? Maybe his mother had something to do with this for the benefit of raising her son's prestige? Can I even depend on Hugh to promote the record-breaking feat that almost claimed both of our lives on more than one occasion? Well, maybe I am making too much of this. I can always enjoy my half of the prize money to set up my next venture to the sky.* On top of all of that, possibly foremost were his thoughts of Diane. *Has she heard of our landing? Will I see her soon?*

With those thoughts he fell fast asleep and did not wake for more than fourteen hours.

52

Diane

That same morning Diane drove through thick fog and arrived at the hospital even before *Miss Veedol* had landed. She had been unable to sleep because she couldn't stop thinking of Clyde and decided it made no sense to lie in bed. After breathing in the cool, crisp autumn air outside, she couldn't help noticing how much the hospital stank. But a nurse needed to get used to the smells and the screams of those in pain and the plaintive moans of the dying. It wasn't always easy, though.

Her colleagues considered Diane a brilliant nurse. She had that special way about her, and all her patients were comforted by her presence. Even the doctors felt she was uniquely gifted. Some even thought she should go to medical school and become a doctor. And she would have loved that, but she put the thought out of her mind because it was something her family could never afford. One thing she was certain of: she could never give up her work because she loved it too much.

It was too early to do rounds, so she went down to the cafeteria to get some breakfast. She hadn't eaten at home, since she didn't want the banging of pots and pans to wake her parents. Like her, they had sat up until after 1:00 a.m. waiting for Clyde's plane to land.

She was hungry, so she ordered a Spanish omelet with toast and coffee. A few minutes after she sat down at a table, her friend Louise joined her.

"I see you're here early too," Louise said.

Diane looked up from her omelet. "I couldn't sleep."

"I bet you were thinking about Clyde Pangborn," Louise said. "Have you heard anything? Has his plane landed? Everyone is talking about it."

Diane shook her head. "No, I haven't heard a thing, and I'm a little worried."

"You care about the guy, don't you?"

"He's a good friend."

Louise shook her head. "I think he means a lot more than that to you."

"I wish everybody would stop telling me how I feel. Besides, it doesn't matter. We aren't right for each other."

Louise put her hand on her friend's arm. "Why do you say that?"

"He loves flying, and I love nursing, and we could never love each other as much as we do our work. Look at my parents—they are a perfect match. They love each other more than anything else. Sure, he enjoys the farm and she has her antiques and her bridge club, but the first order of business with them is each other. It would never be that way with me and Clyde."

Diane wanted to take a walk before it was time to start rounds. She kissed Louise on the cheek and went outside and away from the hospital grounds. She thought that if she walked she might get rid of this terrible feeling of hopelessness. Until she had spoken the words to Louise, she had harbored the hope that things might work out between her and Clyde. Now she knew that they wouldn't, and she was sadder than she had been in a long time.

At the end of the next street, the wind hit her full force, making her coat whip around her. She hung her head low, thinking of the struggle Clyde must be enduring. Then she caught her breath and headed back to the hospital, suddenly feeling better with the thought of her patients.

When she walked inside the hospital, half the staff was standing in the lobby, and she wondered what had happened. Even Dr. Garrison was among them. Louise pushed her way through the crowd and threw her arms around Diane.

"They made it!"

Diane's mouth became an O of surprise. "You mean it? They landed?"

Louise nodded. "They announced it on the radio not more than ten minutes ago. Oh, and you're late for rounds."

Tears were streaming down her cheeks. "I am? My watch must have stopped."

"Don't worry about that," Dr. Garrison said. "Jeanne is going to cover for you. If you leave now, you can be in Seattle by tomorrow for the recognition and celebration event."

53

Seattle Celebration

The day of the landing, the wings were removed from *Miss Veedol* and were prepared to be trucked to Seattle for repair. While waiting for parts, Mrs. Boardman was paid to display the airplane in downtown Seattle in a realistic crash setting at the local Bon Marche store.

Hugh, serving as the flight spokesman, explained that after flying over Seattle, they flew past Mount Rainer, and then toward Boise before weather turned them back toward Spokane, where that area was as well fogged in. After that, they tried Pasco in the tri-cities area before they finally diverted to Wenatchee, which turned out to be the only region with acceptable landing weather. This all added another four and one half hours of flying time after passing over Seattle.

A press conference was planned for the day after that in Seattle. During that event, Hugh's mother would formally accept the prize money and undoubtedly recognize the two fliers.

Clyde and Hugh were also en route to Seattle to obtain formal recognition for their historic flight. They had just arrived at the reviewing stand in front of city hall when Clyde spotted Diane. She was working her way through the crowd.

He yelled, "Diane, over here!"

She looked in his direction and immediately broke into tears. "Clyde, I was worried sick. You made it! You made it!"

As they approached, they both opened their arms to grasp each other in extreme happiness and joy. They hugged each other tightly as their lips joined for the first time. Both realized their love had been brewing ever since their brief visit at the hospital three months ago.

Clyde told her, "Come on, stay with me. I think we are going to have an exciting time." He held her around her waist as he guided her toward the podium. "I've got a special place for you—right beside me."

More investigation went into the prize money that the two might claim. The Japanese *Asabi Shimbum* newspaper award of twenty-five thousand dollars was the only one that was 'for sure' and Mrs. Boardman already had the check in possession. The twenty-eight thousand dollar prize offered by the Seattle business people said the flight departed too far from Tokyo and landed too far from Seattle; some also claimed the flight was to be made westbound rather than eastbound. The one-stop Dallas prize was offered to only those pre-selected by Colonel Easterwood—and the *Miss Veedol* effort wasn't under consideration.

Even then, Clyde considered that his half of the prize money would put him in good shape for setting up his next flying venture. He wasn't sure what that venture would be yet as he hadn't had the opportunity to digest the extreme feat he had just completed.

A crowd of people gathered to witness the event and to see first-hand the famous fliers. There were reporters from all over the region representing the major papers from the northwest, including those from Seattle, Portland, Spokane, and Boise. Alice Boardman arrived the night before to formally accept the prize money. The reporters had already toured the landing sight in Wenatchee and were told that *Miss Veedol* was being trucked to Seattle for repair and then would be flown to New York by the same two men so that they could complete their around-the-world trip. After that, the ownership would be transferred over to new owners who planned to use her for a trans-Atlantic flight.

After being introduced, Mrs. Boardman said, "I am humbled and honored to be here today and to be recognized as having played a role in achieving the first nonstop Pacific crossing. I can only do so by first recognizing the two brave men who were instrumental in the flight. First, my son, Hugh, took on the tremendous risks and provided the knowledge to see the mission through. But he could not have done it alone. His good friend Clyde Pangborn was a faithful assistant all the way to their successful arrival in Wenatchee. For this I award him his share of the proceeds. I have here a check for twenty-five hundred dollars to compensate him for his services."

Very upset by this so-called recognition, Clyde maintained his composure and gratefully accepted the check. He never anticipated in his wildest dreams that he would be treated in this way by Hugh and his mother. Still thinking there must be some mistake, he raced back to his quarters to study the papers Hugh had thrown in front of him to sign during the flight preparation. There he discovered that some of the papers contained the process that would be used in calculating the fifty-fifty proceeds split. It was to be a split in the profits and not a fifty-fifty split of the prize money as earlier discussed.

Dejected, Clyde had already experienced that life had its ups and downs. This had become a giant down but one that must be overcome. At least he had set a major record in aviation, and nobody could ever take that away from him. Besides, he was once again safe on the ground in America and with his best girl, Diane. The two of them decided to celebrate with dinner out in one of the finest restaurants in Seattle.

54

The Trip to New York

Within a few weeks, *Miss Veedol* was repaired and cleared to make the flight to New York. It was possibly the longest flight Clyde had ever taken, as all communications with Hugh pertained to the flight. There was never a bit of humor or a smile between the two during the entire flight. Once arriving, they were greeted by the Mayor of New York and given a key to the city as was always done at such special events. Clyde was impressed but could hardly wait to return to Washington State, Diane, and his family.

Once the events concluded, Clyde made plans to immediately rush back to Wenatchee. He shook Hugh's hand and thanked him for the experiences they shared together. That was the last face to face association that Clyde ever had with Hugh and his family. He had accomplished his goal in life but planned to continue his career in the aviation field in more congenial circles.

During his time away, Clyde was not aware of activities being conducted by his brother Percy and his 'girlfriend' Diane. They had both decided that Clyde had had enough of this dangerous life and had better settle down to a more relaxed environment. Percy was fairly well-off as his jewelry business in Wenatchee had been successful for many years. He told Diane that he would buy Clyde a large spread in the mountains surrounding Wenatchee where he could farm, hunt, fish, and target practice. They found just the right place and planned to surprise Clyde with it when he returned.

Diane dreamed of spending her life with Clyde in this beautiful, remote location. They named it "The Hummingbird Ranch," as the wild flowers were so profuse that they attracted humming birds by the thousands. The eye could barely see the herd of horses as they frolicked in the meadows against the far ridge. Percy had spent several hours down at the creek fishing for the native rainbow trout that hatched from eggs two years earlier. Deer, elk, and birds of all types frequented the area to complete the perfect picture of nature.

The two were at the train station to welcome Clyde upon his return. Although he was very tired and weary from the trip, he was excited to see Percy and particularly Diane who he had longed for since leaving for New York six days earlier. They didn't say anything about the spread but told Clyde that they had something to show him and discuss with him in the morning after he had time to rest.

They all went to Percy's house to have dinner and spend the night. Clyde and Diane did not go to bed but snuggled all night on the dual porch swing. During breakfast the next morning, Percy and Diane told Clyde about the "Hummingbird Ranch" in the mountains that Percy bought while he was in New York and suggested they drive out there after breakfast.

They drove for an hour through the forests up the White River above Wenatchee. When they arrived, they were excited to see Clyde's reaction. Percy suggested they do some target practice with their pistols right there against the old pine tree on the edge of the meadow. Clyde remarked, "I don't want anything to do with those things. The last time I saw one Ivan Gates emptied it at me in a fit of rage."

Figure 26. Clyde, Brother Percy and Mother Opal discuss Clyde's future

Then Percy presented him with the plan. "This place is yours as long as you want it. You had more than your share of excitement for any lifetime and it is time to slow down and enjoy life."

Clyde was perplexed and knew he was in no condition to make any major decision at this time. He didn't consider himself old and was in no way about to put himself out to pasture. The thought of settling down in such a peaceful place and spending all of his time somewhere so beautiful with Diane was really tempting. On the other hand, he was born to fly.

55

Rosalie Meets Clyde Again

It had been eight years since Clyde experienced his ordeal in Houston with the young parachutist, Rosalie Gordon. Since that time, she had married a young Lawyer by the name of Mark Richardson and given birth to a set of twins. She had always felt a certain attachment to Clyde Pangborn as being pivotal during one of the most stirring times of her life, when she was almost killed by an airplane. She was a strong-willed person, however, and let the trying time wane from being number-one in her memory. Clyde's attempt at the record of a nonstop Pacific crossing was of keen interest to her.

She was very excited about the safe landing Clyde Pangborn made in some little farm town called Wenatchee, Washington. It was nearing spring, and Rosalie thought it might be a good time for the family to take a vacation together. She proposed the idea to her husband Mark, and he was quite receptive. His current law case had just resolved, and he hadn't been given a new one. He thought they could afford to take one or two weeks off to spend with the family.

Typically this time of year, Rosalie and Mark liked to travel to the hot country, but Houston was quite hot for this time of year, and they needed to cool off.

"You know, Mark, I've never been to the Pacific Northwest, such as Washington, Oregon, and Idaho," Rosalie said. "And that area has became quite well-known in the past months because of Clyde Pangborn's Pacific crossing.

Mark replied, "You're right. I have never been to that area, myself. It would be good to go up there and explore the region. The kids might enjoy it as well. I'm sure it is quite different than the flat country we have around here."

Within two weeks, they found themselves in Seattle, about four months after the big Pangborn/Herndon celebration. They visited the waterfront and saw where a new fledgling airplane manufacturer by the name of William Boeing was starting construction on some sort of airliner concept. Boeing had just joined several other companies to form a single company by the name of United Airlines. The company planned to offer a trip clear across the U.S. that would take only twenty-seven hours! While in the area, the Richardson's took a tour on a boat around the Puget Sound islands. To the southwest, high above them towered Mount Rainier. It was hard to believe that Clyde and this guy Hugh Herndon almost ran into it on their return to the U.S.

As a day trip, Rosalie and Mark agreed to travel to Wenatchee over the Cascades. They wanted to visit the now-famous landing site of the *Miss Veedol*. It was a beautiful trip over Stevens Pass to Wenatchee. Snow had fallen earlier that night but melted on the roadway so that travel was no problem. They stopped on the pass to let the twins play in the snow for their very first time.

Then they traveled down the hill eastward to Wenatchee. They first passed through miles of barren sagebrush country before reaching a number of well-cultivated apple orchards. Once through the town of Wenatchee, they took a small ferry across the Columbia River to the east side.

They were lost. Stopping at what seemed to be the single gas station in the area, they asked for directions to Fancher Field—the airstrip where *Miss Veedol* landed. They were told to pass through the opening in the fence a mile further down the road and take the dirt sagebrush "path" up the hill.

"Are you going up there in that car?" the attendant asked.

"We thought so. Is there a problem?"

"No, not if you take it easy. Just plan to take your time. You'll be alright."

So on they traveled, up the single-lane dirt sagebrush road to Fancher Field. The dust was six inches deep.

When they arrived, they were surprised to see they weren't alone. At least half dozen cars had arrived there ahead of them. They walked into the hanger to ask directions.

"Oh, the airstrip is up the hill from here. Be sure to stay alert up there and watch the kids. We don't want any accidents."

Rosalie, Mark, and the two kids began their trudge up the hill. They noticed several other people up there apparently surveying the scene as they intended to do. They were grouped together and one man seemed to be giving them a lecture.

As they approached, the speaker looked at them and said, "Rosalie? Rosalie Gordon, is that you?"

Rosalie was surprised but thought that she vaguely recognized the man from a distance.

"I'm Clyde Pangborn," he said. "Didn't we have an event together some years ago in Houston?"

"Yes, yes," she said and began to move in his direction.

He opened his arms and gave her a big hug. "How in the hell are you? By gosh you're looking great!"

"I am. I read all about your adventures—it must have been exciting."

"It was. It was one of two events in my career that were the most exciting things that I'd encountered as a pilot: this trip and the time we had to rescue a performing parachutist over Houston," he quipped. "But what about you, what are you up to these days?"

"Well, my name isn't Rosalie Gordon anymore. It's Rosalie Richardson. This is my husband, Mark," she said as she placed her hand on his upper arm. "We have twins. This is Elizabeth, and this is Jason. Elizabeth had a little accident a few weeks ago and burnt her hand, that is why it is all bandaged up—but she is doing fine now. How does it happen that we found you here today, Clyde?"

"This spot is very dear to me. I expect that I'll stop here often over the next number of years—just like I do at the farm in the Houston area. These places become so ingrained in my mind that I have to visit them on occasion."

"Well, it is amazing that we were able to meet again," Rosalie said.

"It sure is, and I'm extremely happy for you. I have to go now, but you'll always have my best wishes," Clyde said as he backed away ready to walk off.

"Best of luck to you, Clyde. I'm so happy that your trip ended so well. Good-bye," she said as he walked down the hill toward the hanger.

"Good-bye, Rosalie," he said. "It was great seeing you again."

Finale

Back in Tokyo

"What a phenomenal story. Why haven't I heard this before?" the more astute older pilot asked. "It certainly gives me a new appreciation for something that we do every day. Whatever happened to Pangborn?"

I told him, "Since his relationship with Hugh was already strained, their partnership quickly dissolved. "Clyde became involved with a number of multi-engine air races. Further as Senior Captain for the Royal Air Force, he made 178 trans-Atlantic flights."

The waitress came by and offered to help every one with their drinks. The aircrew couldn't partake but offered me a sake—apparently in appreciation for the story. She was given a polite, "No Thanks".

"Pangborn flew every type of multi-engine aircraft used during the war. During that time, he also recruited American fliers for the Royal Air Force by helping them enter Canada where they could legally enlist to fight for the British."

"How did that work?" asked one of the pilots

I had to admit I didn't really know but, "many things are possible during war time."

"He later joined the RAF Ferry Command, where he played a key role in ferrying war

Figure 27. WWII Bomber delivered by Pangborn

equipment across the Atlantic to England. It was during this time that he delivered more than 170 airplanes to the Allies."

"He didn't become a commercial airline pilot, like you guys, until later on. He worked to pioneer flight paths and developed airplane concepts. Sort of a test pilot I'd say."

Right then, the loud speaker blared, "LAST CALL FOR BOARDING ALL NIPPON FLIGHT 66 TO LOS ANGELES, LAST CALL."

The pilots ordered another round of sodas. They were ready to settle down for a summary of this guy.

"Ultimately, he amassed more than twenty-four thousand flying hours. During that time, he never had an accident or injured a passenger."

In all, the pilots listened in rapt attention and seemed very impressed by Clyde Pangborn and what he had accomplished.

"He remained single except for a two-year period when he married a lady from France. There he experienced first-hand how difficult it was to maintain a passion for aviation and have a healthy home life in those days.

"Another interesting fact is that during his record flight he carried the first piece of airmail ever to cross the Pacific."

"He died on March 29, 1958; never having received the accolades awarded other early-day flying heroes. His accomplishments, however, didn't go totally unnoticed. He was honored with American aviation's prestigious Harmon Trophy—joining other greats such as Charles Lindbergh and Jimmy Doolittle. And news came from Japan that he

had been forgiven for his earlier violations and that he had been awarded the Imperial Aeronautical Society's White Medal of Merit. He was buried with full military honors at Arlington National Cemetery."

"Does anyone understand why Clyde did not achieve the attention he deserves?" asked the older pilot.

"It is not clear why this great achievement was not better

Courtesy of the Wenatchee Valley Museum and Cultural Center #000.50.133

recognized. Possibly the gag order placed on Clyde by Hugh prevented further advertising of the accomplishment. Fanfare that might have developed a year later after the gag order expired would have fallen flat as new accomplishments happened in rapid succession in those days. For example, Amelia Earhart was married during that year. You might say that Clyde and Hugh's feat was a flight to nowhere. Lindbergh didn't fly to Paris because he wanted to go to Paris. He went there for the fanfare, the prestige, and to hold the record of being the first solo flight to cross the Atlantic. Pangborn similarly didn't fly to Wenatchee because he wanted to go to Wenatchee. He too wanted to be an aviation hero—but his accomplishment fell short of its goal."

"What was there then that signifies this great achievement?"

"Possibly, the most memorable gesture following the record breaking flight of *Miss Veedol* was a gift from the people of Wenatchee to the people of Misawa City. In response to the unique gift of five apples he received from the small Japanese boy before takeoff, Clyde arranged for the mayor of Wenatchee to send to his counterpart in Misawa City, five cuttings from Washington State's renowned Richard or Red Delicious apples. They have since been grafted onto trees throughout Japan and are currently served in prestigious restaurants—the apples are the same as the ones that you are eating right now."

One pilot bit into an apple. "They're delicious," he said. The other pilots laughed.

"Diane Bronson supported Clyde's decision to continue flying, but she had ambitions of her own. She moved back to Boise, where she continued her nursing career and was very successful. Her thoughts of the excitement of being married to a flier became less frequent. A number of years later she married a surgeon and the two of them moved to the Methow Valley located about fifty miles north of Wenatchee. There they bought a sixty-acre remote ranch surrounded by pine forests and wildlife, similar to the one she had almost lived on with Clyde.

Right then, I had to sneeze, I quickly grabbed my hankie and covered my face. "Achew! Excuse me! I don't know what brought that on?"

"Clyde's travels often brought him to Asia. He looked for Yumiko and her father, Yosh, on several occasions. But he gave up his search when he found that Yosh and his family were sent to Nagasaki earlier to aide in their war effort.

I took my hankie and wiped my face some more.

217

"Later, when World War II broke out, Hugh Herndon became a captain in the Royal Canadian Air Force, ferrying bombers. Afterwards, he became chief pilot of the Africa-Middle East region for Transcontinental and Western Airline, which later became known as the Trans World Airline. He died of a stroke in 1947 in Cairo, Egypt, at an early age of fifty while serving as regional director of operations for TWA. He was married twice. He divorced Mary Ellen Farley, who he had married just prior to the 1931 trip. They had two girls together. He later remarried a lady by the name of Ruth Dainty.

Then one of the pilots blurted out, "But whatever happened to the airplane—the famous *Miss Veedol*."

"Oh, yes, and we mustn't forget *Miss Veedol*. She is no longer with us either. After our two heroes flew her to New York, her ownership was transferred to new owners, who wanted to use her for trans-Atlantic flights. She was eventually renamed *The American Nurse*, painted white, and departed Floyd Bennett Field in New York for Rome in June of 1932. From there, she was never heard from again. The only part of her that remains is her propeller she bent in the sagebrush. It resides in the Wenatchee Valley Museum and Cultural Center along with other displays of the Pangborn era.

"Now, can you believe this," I said. "A year and a half after they landed, a wheel was found washed up on a beach at Cape Flattery at the Northwest tip of Washington State. It was proven to be one of the wheels jettisoned from *Miss Veedol* near Japan. It apparently was carried by the Japanese current some forty-four hundred miles and ended up only two hundred miles from where the record-breaking flight ended. The wheel was lost as quickly as it was found. The whereabouts of this wheel today remains a mystery."

Bibliography

Aviation Firsts—Delaware (web information), http://www.dot.state. mn.us/aero/aved/museum/aviation_firsts/delaware.html

Clyde Edward Pangborn Papers, Washington State University Libraries (Material Source), Cage 112, 1918-1958, Approximate Number of Items: 9550

Clyde Pangborn, Dare Devil (web information), The National Aviation Hall of Fame. http://www.nationalaviation.org/pangborn-clyde/

Clyde Edward Pangborn (web information), Wikipedia, http:// en.wikipedia.org/wiki/Clyde_Edward_Pangborn

Clyde Pangborn belly-lands a monoplane in Wenatchee (web information), HistoryLink.org, http://www.historylink.org/index.cfm? displaypage=output.cfm&file_id=5400

First Across the Pacific, Non-Stop, HistoryNet.com, Terry Gwynn-Jones, September 23, 1998   http://www.historynet.com/first-across-the-pacific-nonstop-november-98-aviation-history-feature.htm

Oct. 5, 1931: First Nonstop Trans-Pacific Flight Ends in Cloud of Dust, This Day in Tech Jason Paur, October 5, 2010   http://www.wired. com/thisdayintech/2010/10/1005first-nonstop-transpacific-flight/

Oct. 5, 1931: First Nonstop Trans-Pacific—(web information), This Day In Tech, http://www.wired.com/thisdayintech/2010/10/1005 first-nonstop-transpacific-flight/

In 1931 Clyde Pangborn—(web information), Aerofiles, http://aero-files.com/missveedol.html

Last Chance for Glory: The incredible story of the first transpacific flight from Japan to East Wenatchee (DVD), Wenatchee Valley Museum

PANG (Brochure), Wenatchee Valley Museum & Cultural Center

Pangborn, Clyde Edward (web information), www.aircrash.org; http://www.aircrash.org/burnelli/pang_bio.htm

Pangborn-Herndon Memorial Site (web information), National Parks Service, http://www.nps.gov/nr/travel/aviation/pan.htm

"Upside-Down" Pangborn: King of the Barnstormers (Book), Cleveland, Carl M., 1978, Glendale: Aviation Book Company

"Upside-Down" Pangborn (VHS Recording), First Across the Pacific, KSPS

Who is Clyde Pangborn (web information), SquidWho, http://www.squidoo.com/clydepangborn

Who was this Hometown hero: Clyde Pangborn (web information), Wrong bridge, October 8, 2006, The Wenatchee World, http://www.wenatcheeworld.com/news/2006/oct/08/who-was-this-hometown-hero-clyde-pangborn/

And *many more*: Just put *Clyde Pangborn* in your favorite search engine.

About the Authors

Edward (Ted) Heikell and Robert (Bob) Heikell are brothers born in Yakima, Washington, and raised in Wapato, Washington, about seventy miles southwest of the town of Wenatchee. Ted was born in 1938. He graduated from Wapato High School and later from the University of Washington with a Bachelor's degree in Aeronautical Engineering. Bob was the oldest of five Heikell children and was born in 1933. He graduated from Wapato High School and then went on to obtain his Masters degree in Education at the Central Washington College of Education in Ellensburg, Washington.

Ted worked for The Boeing Company in Seattle for thirty-four years in both their commercial and military divisions. He ended up being the proposal manager and technology manager for a prestigious military contract. His leisure time was mostly spent hiking, skiing, fishing, hunting. He also enjoyed flying in his spare time and was a part owner of a Cessna 182 for fifteen years. Since his retirement in 1996, he obtained his commercial instrument license but later got out of private flying as he advanced in age. This is his first attempt at literature, but he has two DVDs on the market pertaining to hunting and fishing.

Bob worked most of his years as the principal of several intermediate and grade schools—primarily in the Moses Lake, Washington, area, which is located about forty miles southeast of the town of Wenatchee. Bob also holds a commercial pilots license. During six of his years since retiring from public schools, he served as the center director for the Embry Riddle Aeronautical University in Moses

Lake. He loves the opportunity to verbally communicate to crowds and organized groups. His leisure time was mostly spent hiking, hunting, flying, and building model airplanes. To aide the Wenatchee annual event with its sister city, Misawa, Japan, Bob built a twelve-foot wingspan radio-controlled model of the *Miss Veedol* airplane, a J-300 Bellanca Long-Distance Special. In doing so, he became more and more familiar with the story of Clyde Pangborn and Hugh Herndon Jr. His model-building skills became quite well-known as he received many national awards for his model's physical and flying accuracy. One of these models hangs from the rotunda dome inside the city hall of East Wenatchee.